CHINNA KATHA - I

Stories and Parables

Quoted from the Divine Discourses of

BHAGAVAN SRI SATHYA SAI BABA

Sri Sathya Sai Sadhana Trust

Publications Division

Prasanthi Nilayam

SRI SATHYA SAI SADHANA TRUST, PUBLICATIONS DIVISION

Prasanthi Nilayam - 515 134

Anantapur District, Andhra Pradesh, INDIA

STD : 08555 ISD : 91-8555

Phone : 287375. Fax : 287236

E-mail: enquiry@sssbpt.org

International Standard Book Number : 978-81-7208-782-1 / 978-81-7208-536-0 (set)

Previously printed by Sri Sathya Sai Books And Publications Trust in April 1999 and February 2000

First Edition: February 2010

Reprint: July 2010 Reprint : August 2012

Published by

The Convener,
Sri Sathya Sai Sadhana Trust, Publications Division
Prasanthi Nilayam, India - Pin Code 515 134
STD : 08555 ISD : 91 - 8555
Phone : 287375 Fax : 287236
E-mail: enquiry@sssbpt.org

Printed at :
Omkar Offset Printers
3/3, 1st Main Road, New Tharagupet,
Bangalore - 560 002
Ph: 2670 8186, 2670 9026
E-mail: omkaroffset@gmail.com
Website : www.omkaroffset.com

FORE WORD

"Oka Chinna Katha"- when Bhagavan intercepts the speeding current of His Discourse with these three Telugu words, meaning ,"One Little Story", all ears are alert, all hearts are quivive. For, the story that follows is a flash that illumines, a shower that cools, a joke that tickles, a 'tablet' that alleviates, a peep into epic grandeur or pompous absurdity, a poetic parenthesis, an exhilarating prick, a lilt that enlightens, a sugar-coated pill of profoundity, a disarming repartee, a volley of raillery on religious rigmarole ! It may be a tonic tale of the past or the report of a contemporary comedy; it may be a thrust on theological disputation or dear little dig at some egoistic dignatary.

The Chinna Katha, if only we ponder over its relevance, is an effective instrument in Bhagavan's educational process. When He is discoursing, these parables and stories, ever on the wing, hover in flocks in the firmament of His Love; He lets a few fly into our hearts and nestle there, until we fondle and foster them and make them part of our thought and behaviour patterns. Here is a charming, fragrant bouquet of these multicoloured Kathas, for our delectation, mediation and inspiration.

The First Collection of "Chinna Katha" was made by members of the Sri Satya Sai Study Circle, Delhi, and the Prasanthi Workshop, Madras, and was published in 1975 by the Sri Sthya Sai Seva Samithi, New Delhi.

Prasanthi Nilayam

Sankranti. 14-1-78 **N. Kasturi**

CONTENTS

STORIES AND PARABLES

CHINNA KATHA -PART I

Stories and Parables

VINAYAKA - THE LEADER OF ALL

On one occasion, a competition was arranged among the Gods for selecting the leader of the Ganas (troops of demigods who are the attendants of Siva). Participants had to go round the world quick and come back to the feet of Lord Siva. The gods started off on their own vehicles; the elder son of Siva also enthusiastically entered the competition. He had an elephantine head; his vehicle was a mouse! Therefore, his progress was severely handicapped. He had not proceeded far, when Narada appeared before him and asked him," Whither are you bound?" The son was very much annoyed; he fell into a rage. For, what happened was a bad omen, doubly unpropitious for those going on a journey. It is inauspicious if the first person you come across when you are on a journey is a 'lone Brahmin'.Though the foremost among the Brahmins (he was the son of Brahma Himself), Narada was a bad omen! Again it is a bad omen if you are going somewhere and someone asks you, "Whither are you bound?". Narada put to him that very question.

Nevertheless, Narada was able to assuage his anger. He drew forth from Siva's son the cause of his predicament and his desire to win. Narada consoled him, exhorted him not to yield to despair, and advised him thus: "Rama - the name- is the seed from which the gigantic tree called the universe has emanated. So, write the name on the ground, go round it once, and hurry back to Siva, claiming the prize." He did so and returned to his Father. When asked how he returned so soon, he related the story of Narada and his advice.

Siva appreciated the validity of Narada's counsel; the prize was awarded to the son, who was acclaimed as Gana-pati, (Master of the Ganas) and Vinayaka (Leader of all).

GURU'S GRACE BRINGS ETERNAL GLORY

Sankara, the great acharya, had four chief pupils: Thotaka, Hastamalaka, Sureswara and Padmapada. Of these, Padmapada was intent only on service to the Guru; he could not pay attention to the lessons. The others used to sneer at him for his backwardness in studies. But his deep reverence for the guru made up for it. One day, he washed the clothes of his Guru and dried them on a rock in the middle of the river; but, even as he was folding them, the river rose fast in a swirling flood; and he had scarce a foot-hold on the top of the rock. It was getting late; the Guru would need the washed clothes soon; so Padmapada resolved to walk across over the raging waters. He knew that the blessing of his Guru would rescue him. It did. Wherever his foot was planted, a sturdy lotus bloomed and bore him on its petals. That is why he came to be called, Lotus-footed, Padmapada ! The grace of the Guru enabled him to master all knowledge and shine as a brilliant exponent of the ancient wisdom.

LIGHTING THE LAMP OF WISDOM

Once a Sadhaka, who had a great ambition to knowsome thing about the divine, wanted his eye of wisdom to be opened. He entered a cave where a guru was residing. While entering the cave he saw a small light. As he moved forward even that little light got extinguished. In darkness one feels frightened, and in fear, we think of God very intensively. Thus he uttered loudly the word 'Namah Sivaya' and on hearing this, the saint asked him who he was. He said that he had come to seek his grace. The great saint, who was sustaining himself in the cave only by breathing the air around him, had the competence to know the mind of his visitor. He said that he will answer his question later but asked him first to go and light the lamp which had just been extinguished. The visitor took a match box and tried to light the lamp but did not succeed. He told the guru that he had finished all the match sticks and yet he had not succeeded in lighting the lamp. The guru asked him to see if there was oil in the lamp. After seeing the lamp, he found that there was no oil and reported to the guru that there was only water in the lamp. The guru then asked him to open the lamp, put out all the water and pour oil in it, and then try to light it. The person did this but the lamp would not light even then. The guru then said that the wick was probably wet with water and asked him to dry it nicely in the open and then attempt to light the lamp. He did this and succeeded. Then the person ventured to mention his need and sought it from the guru. The surprised guru said that the appropriate answer was being given all the while. The visitor pleaded that, being an ignorant man he was not able to understand the significance of the teaching and requested the guru to explain to him in clearer terms. The guru said: In the vessel of your heart, there is the wick of your jiva. That wick has been immersed all these days in the water of your sensuous desires. Therefore you are not able to light the lamp of wisdom. Pour out all the water of desires from the vessel of your heart, and fill it with namasmarana of God. Take the wick of jiva and dry it in the bright sunshine of vairagya; squeeze out of it all the water present in the form of desire and put, into the heart, the oil of devotion or namasmarana. It will then be possible for you to light the lamp of wisdom.

THE LORD HAS NO FIXED FORM

There was an artist who had travelled far and wide and had built up for himself an extensive reputation. But so far he had not achieved access to Krishna ! As such he was anxious to seek approbation from Lord Krishna as well. With this view, one day he got an appointment with Krishna, met Him and requested him to stay still, so that he could paint His picture. He prepared the outline and told Krishna that he would get ready with the final painting in a week's time. Krishna knew the ego of the painter. After a week, the painter brought a finished portrait, covered with a white cloth. In Krishna's presence, when he uncovered the painting, the painter himself was shocked at the lack of similarity between Krishna and the painting. The painter was completely surprised and asked for a week's time to get the job done. The painter tried several times but every time the result was equally disappointing. In complete frustration and total dejection, he wanted to leave the city and go away. When he was going away, sage Narada met him. Narada told him that it was silly to attempt to paint the picture of Lord Krishna. The Lord has no fixed form and he can change His face every second. Narada advised, "If you do want to paint Him, I will tell you a method which will enable you to do so." Narada whispered some thing into the ear of the artist. Following the advice given by Narada, the painter came back, with a white cloth covering some thing and again approached Krishna and told Him that this time, He is welcome to change in any manner but the painting will look exactly like Him. When the cloth was removed, Krishna saw only a mirror and this mirror produced an exact replica of Krishna. If, therefore, you are imagining that God is like this or like that, it is not correct. You cannot describe God and your attempts will fail. Make your mind clear and clean, fill it with love and devotion; that will enable you to have the true vision of God.

THE SACRED FRUITS OF ACTION

On a Saturday, a father was involved in worshipping the Lord and he called his son and told him to get some plantains for one rupee. This son was a good boy; he purchased the plantains, but on the way he saw a mother and son, who were very hungry, standing on the road. When the hungry boy saw the plantains he ran towards them. The hungry mother who saw the boy running, ran after him and caught him but both of them collapsed of hunger. When this young man found these people suffering so much from hunger, he thought that it was much better to feed hungry people than take the bananas home. He gave the bananas to this mother and son and later brought water and gave it to them. These people were so relieved of their hunger and thirst that they expressed their gratitude in many different ways and shed tears of joy. This young student went home empty handed and when the father asked him if he had brought the bananas, he replied in the affirmative. When asked where the bananas were, the son replied that the bananas he brought were sacred, would not rot and could not be seen. The son explained that he fed two hungry souls with the bananas and the fruits which he brought home are only the sacred fruits of the action. The father then felt that his son was worthy of him and he felt that all his prayers had been answered that day. The father developed great affection for the son from that day and they came much closer to each other.

DOUBLE THE PRICE

An individual took a watch which was out of order to a watch-repairer. The watch - repairer said that the watch was very old and that it would cost a lot of money to repair the watch. He said that repair would cost at least two times the original price of the watch. The owner said that he would like the watch to be repaired even if it costs so much. The watch-repairer thought that, since the owner was insisting on this old and worn-out watch being repaired the watch was probably a lucky one. He replaced the old parts by new parts, repaired the watch and gave it back to the owner. When asked to pay the price of repair, the owner gave two slaps to the watch-repairer. The persons standing by handed him over to the police and when the police asked him to explain why he beat the watch-repairer, he said that he was asked to pay for the repair of the watch twice the price he paid originally when he aquired the watch and since he did not purchase it but got it by giving one slap to a person, he gave two slaps to the repairer!

THE BEST GIFT TO ASK FROM GOD

Our faith diminishes because our ambitions are limitless. There was a rich person who had a daughter with a flat nose. The father wanted to get this girl married. Every person who came and looked at the girl used to go away, although they were tempted by the wealth. In those days, persons who could perform plastic surgery were not available. In desperation, he announced that he would give plenty of money to anyone who would marry the girl. He somehow found some one to marry her. The marriage was performed, and thereafter the couple developed considerable faith in God. They visited many temples, went on many pilgrimages and bathed in many sacred rivers. They met a saint who advised them that he, who created the nose, alone can bring it back to normal. Although they had lot of wealth, they were not happy at all. The girl used to feel others were looking at her and making fun. She suggested to her husband that they should both go to the lonely Himalayas and spend a month there in that manner. He agreed and they did so. The girl had a great desire to get back her nose, so she began to pray to God in great earnestness. God appeared, due to her good luck, and asked her what she wanted. As soon as God appeared, she asked for the grant of a good looking big nose. God said, so shall it be and granted her the boon. As soon as God disappeared, she looked at her face. She looked at the big nose and felt that she had become uglier than before. She prayed again more earnestly and God appeared again and asked her what she wanted. She said that she did not want that big nose. God said, so shall it be and granted her the boon. She immediately found that her nose had completely disappeared. The moral of this story is that although God is present before you, playing with you and talking with you, you do not know what to ask.

EVERY ONE MUST HAVE FAITH IN HIMSELF

There is no one who does not love himself, has no belief in himself and has no ambition to rise higher and higher. Even a man who does not have faith in God has faith in himself and desires to have the strength by which to cultivate faith in himself. There was once a guru communicating wisdom to people who came for his darshan with flowers and fruits. One day, as the offerings were plenty, he called a disciple and asked him to cut the fruits and arrange for their distribution as prasad. The disciple reported to the guru that all was ready for distribution and asked him who should be given first. The guru asked him to start with the person in whom he has the greatest faith and highest confidence. All the people assembled there thought that the disciple would first give the fruit to the teacher and then distribute to the others. But the disciple did not do so. He took the first fruit himself. When the surprised onlookers asked for explanation he said that since he had the greatest confidence and affection for himself, he took the first fruit.

EXCESS WEALTH CAN CHANGE ONE'S QUALITY

There is a small story which tells us how the possession of wealth will change the qualities of some people . A mother had only one son and a lot of money. The boy had lost his father early in life. As the boy grew older and older, he got into bad company. If the tank is full, frogs gather but once the tank is dried up, all the frogs disappear. Many friends will gather round you so long as you have wealth and the moment wealth disappears, the friends will also disappear without telling you. The son of that wealthy person accumulated a large number of bad friends. He used to go to the mother day after day and demand large sums of money, with the result that the mother's affection towards the boy began diminishing and she developed positive hatred towards the boy. As days went on, the boy lost all attachment to the mother. She thought that it is much better that such a son who brings down the honour and reputation of the parents dies rather than lives and therefore she worked out a plan one day. At the same time, the son had his own plan as he thought the mother was coming in his way. He therefore thought that it is better that such a mother dies rather than lives. One day the son was to kill his mother with an iron rod as the mother came to serve him food. The mother also decided to kill the son the same day by poisoning his food. When the mother came to serve him food, the son hit with the iron rod and killed her. A few minutes later, the boy also died after eating the poisoned food.

SELFISHNESS WILL NEVER WORK IN MATTERS RELATING TO GOD

There is a small story in the Mahabharata. With view to get Krishna on her side, Satyabhama, one of His consorts, went to Narada and requested him to tell her some way, a short-cut by which she can achieve her objective. Narada knew that Satyabhama was very selfish and that selfishness will never work in matters relating to God. Narada wanted to teach a lesson to Satyabhama and said he knew of a method which would get Krishna on her side, a ritual in which she gives away as a gift to someone and then buys Him back by paying money, equivalent in weight to the weight of the Lord. Narada said that Krishna will belong solely to Satyabhama under all circumstances if she went through this ritual. Satyabhama was lured into the plan. Therefore, she did the ritual of gifting Krishna to Narada and then getting Him back. In one pan of the balance, she made Krishna sit and she put all her jewels in the other pan but it was no match to the weight of Krishna. Narada saw an excellent opportunity in the situation and told Satyabhama that since she is not able to give gold needed to equal her husband's weight, he was taking away Krishna and that from that day, Krishna would not belong to her; He would belong to him. In that situation, Satyabhama thought of Rukmini and went in search of her. She found her performing Tulasi pooja. Rukmini went with a few Tulasi in her hand. She was astonished to find that Satyabhama was trying to outweigh the Lord himself with gold. She knew that this would never be possible. She said that gold will never outweigh god and only God's name can match Him in weight. Narada did not agree with this and asked that since Krishna has a form which can be seen, He must be weighed against something which can also be seen. Rukmini immediately grasped the situation and she told herself that whether it is fruit, flower, or a leaf or even a spoon of water if given in full faith, God will surely respond. If there is any truth in this, she expected Krishna to respond to what she was going to do and in full faith, she placed a Tulasi leaf on the other pan of the balance, uttering the name of Krishna. It is only with affection, love and pure heart that one can get God. She won.

ONE STEADY DISCIPLE IS BETTER THAN THOUSAND WAVERING ONES

We know that King Janaka, even while performing ordinary worldly duties like ruling the kingdom and looking after the needs of the kingdom, found it possible to turn his thoughts completely towards the divine. The great Rushi Suka was once teaching several things to his disciples in a forest quite close to Mithilapura. Janaka learnt about this and wanted himself to become a disciple of Suka and listen to his teachings. Janaka went to the forest, made obeisance to Suka and asked that he be accepted as one amongst the numerous disciples Suka had, and requested for permission to attend the classes. From that day, Janaka was conducting himself as one of the disciples. One day when he did not arrive in time, Suka did not start his class and waited till Janaka arrived. He further told the other disciples that he was delaying the class for that reason. When the sage told the other disciples to wait till Janaka arrived, they murmured amongst themselves and told each other that they had joined this great sage only because it was believed that he attached no special importance to kings and other powerful people. From that day, their faith in the guru started weakening. They also became envious of king Janaka.

As soon as Suka saw much envy and jealousy among his disciples, he decided to teach them a lesson. At an opportune moment, all the disciples were made to feel that the entire city of Mithialpura was in flames. Then each one of them began to think of the consequences, of the effect it could have on their houses, and ran to the city to salvage what they can. But king Janaka did not waver or move from his place. Suka told Janaka that the flames appeared to have spread to the palace and he asked Janaka to go and save the inmates of the palace. Janaka was only smiling, thinking that god's will shall be done and no one can change it. The envious students who ran to the city found that there were no flames at all and it was only a make-believe. They came back and reported this to Suka. They expressed surprise at the steady mind of Janaka. Suka looked at the disciples who were envious and told them that it is better to have one disciplined student rather than many who have no stability of mind.

THE THREE BEST THINGS

A king used to ask three questions of all people who came to him. The first question was: who is the best of persons? The second was: what is the best time? And the third: what it is the best of all actions? The king was very anxious to know the answer to these questions . One day, he went to the forest and was moving about the hills and plains. He saw an 'ashram' and wanted to take some rest there. By the time the king reached the 'ashram' , a sadhu was watering some plants. The sadhu saw that the king was rather tired; stopped watering the plants; ran up to the king and gave him some fruits and cool water. At that time, an individual wounded all over the body was brought to the 'ashram' by another sadhu. As soon as the sadhu saw this, he went to the individual. cleaned all his wounds and gave him some herbs which could cure the wounds. He was also telling him sweet words which could console the person. The king wanted to express his gratitude and take leave of him. The sadhu blessed the king but the king was still troubled by his three questions and wanted to see if the sadhu could enlighten him on that matter. The sadhu stated that the answer to the three questions were contained in the actions which the king had witnessed in the 'ashram'. The sadhu said that when the king came to the 'ashram' he was watering the plants and that was his duty. At that time, on seeing the king the sadhu had given up his duty and come to the king and gave him water and fruit. This was in accordance with correct traditions, as the king was his guest. While reliving the king of his thirst and suffering, another injured individual had come to the ashram' and therefore the sadhu had given up the duty of serving the king and went to the other individual and began serving him. Whoever comes seeking service from you is the best individual at that time. Whatever satisfaction you can give him by serving him will be the best work you can do. The present, when you can do something is the most sacred of all times.

HOW TO DEAL WITH A BAD HABIT

One got into the habit of eating opium. It was not possible for him to control this habit. He was always in a kind of coma. A saintly person visited his city and was offering advice and comfort to many. The opium eater also sought the advise of the saint. The saint said that his health was deteriorating and that he should give up eating opium. At this, the opium addict said that it was not possible for him to give it up. He requested the saint to give him some advice. The saint asked him how much of opium he used to take every day and was shown a certain lump as the quantity being taken everyyday. The saint got a piece of chalk, equal to the lump of opium and told him that he may continue eating opium but should not take more than the weight of the chalk each day. The opium eater was quite happy but he was also told that everyday he should write 'OM' three times on a blackboard with that chalk. In this manner, the chalk was reduced in size everyday and so the amount of opium which the person was eating also got reduced gradually and ultimately this habit was removed.

MATHRU BHAKTHI MUST PRECEDE ISWARA BHAKTHI

The first and foremost of my direction is : Revere your paents especially the mother. There was once a place, which was hit by a hurricane so wild that all the houses were razed to the ground, and people had nothing to eat and nowhere to lay their heads. Among the worst hit were a mother and her two sons. The elder boy was a gem of virtue; he felt responsible for the safety and care of the family; he loved his mother, and sought to win her love and blessings, more than anything else.

The mother with the younger child was going out begging and keeping alive on the little they could get from the famine-stricken land. Soon , she found that she was too weak even to walk a few steps and so, the elder son had to go abegging, begging, all alone, to feed the family. He said, falling at her feet, he would do what she was doing and collect food for all. He wanted that she should not over-exert, and worsen her health. How could three live on mere handfuls? The son too was rendered weak. With faint voice and fainter steps, he moved towards a Zamindar's house and called out for a morsel. The lady of the house called him in and led him in and led him to a plate wherein she served some food. But, he tottered into an upright position, and fell plump on the floor. The zamindar came running into the room and placed his ear near the dying boy's mouth, so that he could catch the last word that emerged from his lips. He was saying, 'No, No ! First she must be given food. My turn comes next'. You may be able to pay back any debt; but, the debt you owe your mother, you never can repay. Those who claim to be devotees of God must have this credential; they must revere the mother.

SELF-CONDEMNATION IS EGOISM

Once, Krishna pretended to be suffering from intense,unbearable headache ! He acted that role quite realistically. He wound warm clothes around His Head and rolled restlessly in bed. His eyes were red and He was in evident distress. The face too appeared swollen and pale. Rukmini, Satyabhama and the other queens rushed about with all kinds of remedies and palliatives. But, they were ineffective. At last, they consulted Narada and he went into the sick room to consult Krishna Himself and find out which drug would cure Him.

Krishna directed him to bring- what do you think the drug was ? - the dust of the feet of a true Bhaktha ! In a trice, Narada manifested himself in the presence of some celebrated Bhakthas of the Lord; but, they were too humble to offer the dust of their feet to be used by their Lord as a drug !

That is also a kind of egoism. "I am low, mean, small, useless, poor, sinful, inferior"- such feelings also are egoistic; when the ego goes, you do not feel either superior or inferior. No one would give the dust wanted by the Lord; they were too worthless, they declared. Narada came back disappointed to the sickbed. Then, Krishna asked him" Did you try Brindavan where the Gopis live?: The queens laughed at the suggestion and even Narada asked in dismay, "what do they know of Bhakthi?" Still, the sage had to hurry thither. When the Gopis heard He was ill and that the dust of their feet might cure Him, without a second thought they shook the dust of their feet and filled his hand with the same. By the time Narada reached Dwaraka, the headache had gone. It was just a five day drama, to teach that self-condemnation is also egoism and that the Lord's command must be obeyed without demur, by all Bhakthas.

DEVOTION OF GOPIS

The Gopis had the highest type of Bhakthi in their hearts. There was Neeraja, for example. She was warned against Krishna, when she came to Brindavan from a distant village as the bride of a Gopa. In spite of all warnings, however, she saw Krishna during the Govardhana Festival and when she saw Him, she surrendered her heart to the lord. She passed through great ordeals on account of this spiritual attachment, but she bore it all with courage. She had seen Krishna first at the foot of the Govardhana Hill, playing sweetly on the flute. So she used to go often to that bower where she first saw Him, to inhale the holy air. She was the foremost among those Gopis who tried to curb the horses that drew Akrura's chariot with Krishna in it, away from Brindavan to Mathura. She suffered silently the separation for years and years, until one day when she was exhausted with the agony, Krishna appeared before her in the selfsame bower, where she was. She had one request to make, she longed to hear the Divine flute, before she died on Krishna's lap. The Lord said, "I have not brought it," but just to grant her the boon, he broke a length of reed from the bower. made it in a trice into a flute and played on it a tune that melted Neeraja's heart into tears, which washed her soul away.

WOMEN ARE MORE DEVOTIONAL THAN MEN

It was her maternal love that prompted her to send her husband Kuchela to the Lord so that her children might get a full meal. She had faith in the lord. Kuchela hesitated and argued that Krishna might not recognise him or remember him, or invite him in or accept his homage. She urged him to give up all doubt and proceed at least as far as the gate of the palaceof Krishna. She was certain that Krishna would call him in, if he took at least that little trouble. Kuchela was so nervous that he could be persuaded to go only up to the gate.

Once it was decided that Kuchela would go, she took from the place where she had hidden it for a rainy day, a quantity of paddy, just a handful she put it in boiling water, took it out, dried it and then, frying it over the fire, she pounded it with a pestle to prepare "beaten rice" that Kuchela said, was Krishna's favourite food, while at school. That was tied to a corner of the cloth worn over the body and he moved on, his fear increasing at every step. Such fear should be absent in the genuine Bhaktha. He must approach the Lord as of right and earn the Grace that is his due.

Of course, the Lord showers His mercy on the Aartha and Arthaarthi, as well as on the Jijnaasu and the Jnani. The Aartha is the person who is ill and suffering; the Arthaarthi is the poverty- stricken who seeks prosperity and fortune. So, He called him in, with overwhelming joy, and reminded him of the happy days at school which they had spent together at the Guru's Feet. and even while Kuchela was squirming to hide the common place offering tied to the corner of his tattered cloth Krishna sought out the stuff and began eating it with great relish. Bhakthi had made it very tasty to the Lord.

It is related that Rukmini Devi held His Hand when He took the third handful and the reason given usually by commentators is that she was afraid all the riches of the Lord would go over to Kuchela if a few more handfuls were taken in by the Lord ! What a silly idea ! As if the riches of the Lord are exhaustible, as if He would care if Bhakthas carried all of it away, as if the Mother of the Universe is stringy in her gifts, this can never be true! The real cause for her holding the Hand of Krishna was, she claimed her share of the offering of the Devoted Heart; she wanted a portion for Herself; it was her right to have a share.

Kuchela left Dwaraka rather disappointed, because He was not given any donation or promise of a donation. He was sad, when he remembered his family and the starving chidren. He was lost in grief and so, he passed his own house without noticing that it had undergone a great change and had become overnight a huge big mansion. His wife, who saw him, called him back and related how suddenly, happiness had been showered upon them by Krishna's grace.

WHOEVER SURRENDERS, RAMA ACCEPTS

God is so merciful that He will come ten steps towards you, if you take one step towards Him. Vibhishana, the brother of Ravana, inquired from Hanuman whether Rama will accept his homage and take him under his protecting shade. He said,"I am the brother of His worst enemy, whom he has vowed to destroy; I am a member of the demonic race; I am unacquainted with the Vedas or Sastras or the rituals of the Aryas." Then Hanuman replied "Oh! you fool ! Do you think He cares for ritual correctitude or family status or scholarship? If so, how could He accept me, a monkey ?" That settled the matterVibhishana was assured of Grace. When he went to Rama later, He asked the elder monkeys around Him whether He could accept Vibhishana into the fold. Of course, He did not need any counsel from anyone. He was never influenced by others. But , still, just to bring them into the picture, He consulted and made a pretence of not having made up His mind yet. When Sugreeva said, 'No' Rama reminded him that he too had come to Him first, giving up his elder brother ! When Lakshmana said that the only treatment he deserved was to be thrown back into Lanka, Rama said, "Yes! I am resolved to crown him as the emperor of the Lanka, after the demise of Ravana." Whoever surrenders, Rama accepts on the spot, without reservations. When someone suggested that Vibhishana should not be promised a Throne, for, Ravana may fall at the feet of the Lord and earn pardon for his iniquity, Rama replied, "In that case, I will hold both hands of Bharatha and beg him to make Vibhishana emperor of Ayodhya, our ancestral domain ; we both, Bharatha and I will spend our time happily in the forests."

THE UNIQUE TREASURES OF MANKIND

It is said that during Kurukshetra battle which eighteen days, Vyasa had his mind torn with contrition, for , the contestants were both of his lineage. So, he could not caste his eyes on the fratricidal carnage ! One day, he was so overcome by remorse that he hastened beyond the blood-soaked plain, where another day's holocaust was about to begin. Hurrying along, he saw a spider scurrying forward on the Ground ! "Why so fast ?" inquired the sage; the spider ran off the road, climbed up an ant hill by its side and from that eminence, it replied, "Know you not that the war chariot of Arjuna is about to pass this way ! If I am caught under its wheels, I am done." Vyasa laughed at this reply; he said, "No eye gets wet when you die ! The world suffers no loss when you are killed ! You leave no vacuum when you disappear." The spider was touched to the quick by this insult . It was shaking with rage. It ejaculated, "How is that? You are a bloated sage ! You feel that if you die, it will be a great loss, whereas I will not be missed at all. I too have wife and children whom I love. I too have a home and a store of food. I too cling to life with as much tenacity as you folk. I have hunger, thirst, grief, pain, joy, delight and the agony of separation from kith and kin. The world is as much in me and for me, as in and for human beings and others."

Vyasa hung his head and moved on in silence, muttering the line, *Saamaanyam ethath pasubhir naraani*, for man and beast and insect and worm, these things are common. But, he told himself. "Enquiry into the Ultimate, yearnig for Beauty, Truth and Goodness, Awareness of the underlying Unity, these attributes of Wisdom are the unique treasures of mankind", and went his way.

ADI SANKARA'S PITHRU BHAKTHI BRINGS DIVINE GRACE

Sankara knew the real meaning of the Vedic words 'Mathru Devo Bhava, Pithru Devo Bhava'. Once when his father left the house, he told his son: "My dear son, I am daily worshipping God and distributing naivedya to all the people. So also in my absence and in the absence of your mother, you will please do like that". Sankara promised to do so without fail. He poured some milk in a cup, put it before the idol of the Goddess and prayed to her: "Mother! Take this milk which I am offering". Though he prayed for a long time, the mother did not take the milk, nor did she appear. He was very much disappointed. He said again, "Mother! You are daily taking the offerings that are given to you by my father. What sin have these hands of mine committed that you are not accepting the offering which I am giving to you ?" He prayed to her earnestly from the innermost depths of his heart. He was prepared to sacrifice even his life and told himself "My father asked me to offer this milk to the Goddess but I am not able to do so because the Goddess is not receiving the offering which I made. It is better that I die". He went out and brought a big stone to kill himself. The mother of the universe is very compassionate and she was very much moved and touched by Sankara's sincerity. She at once appeared before him and drank the milk that he offered. She drank the whole milk and placed the empty cup before him. The boy was very glad that the mother of the universe came and drank the milk but there was nothing in the cup to distribute to others. He thought that his father would certainly ask for the naivedya of the God after his return. He feared that the father may think that he drank away all the milk and may be angry with him. Therefore he prayed to the Goddess, "Goddess; give me atleast a drop of milk so that I may be able to give it to my father". But the Goddess did not come. He again sincerely continued to pray ; the Goddess was moved and she again appeared. Because she was not able to give the milk that she drank, she gave her own milk and filled the cup. There is a belief that because Sankara tasted the

Divine milk, he was able to attain the highest learning knowledge and wisdom that is ever possible. So the essence of the Grace of the Goddess became the essence of the learning of Sankara. In order to please his father, he tried hard and was able to get the Goddess of the Universe to manifest Herself before him. From this story, we must learn to revere and obey the orders of our fathers implicitly and sincerely.

THE BLANKET OF MAYA AND THE BEAR

The Atma tathwa is one indivisible. On the bank of a river, once a group of children were tending their cows. It was the mansoon and all of a sudden a furious current of water developed. Because it was a fast current, one Bear which slipped into water was drawn into the midstream and was being carried away. One of the boys looked at the floating mass, and from a distance, it appeared to him to be a bundle of blankets floating in the water. He said to his companions,"I shall jump into the water and get the bundle of blankets out", and so he jumped into the water. With the mistaken idea that it is a bundle of blankets the boy embraced with his hands the bear. Then the bear also embraced him with its own hands. However much the boy tried to extricate himself, the bear did not leave him. It held him fast. The boys on the shore shouted: "Oh my dear companion, leave the bundle and you come away". The boy in the water, struggling to escape, cried out, "Though I want to escape from it , it does not allow me to escape". So in this river of life, Maya plays like the bear and we mistake it to be a bundle of blankets. Hoping that it would offer us solace, comfort and happiness, we jump into the river and try to catch it. At a later stage when we want to extricate ourselves from it, we find it impossible to do so. This illusion is created by Maya but the divine principle is always one.

Visishtadvaita has been teaching from time immemorial that though the forms are different, there is only one purusha, which is the unity in the diversity and multiplicity of forms.

TENALI RAMAKRISHNA'S TANESHA BHARATAM

With a view to use the sacred story of the Pandavas for some material purpose the Taneshah of Delhi once invited to his court the eight renowned poets of Vijayanagar. These poets were asked to describe the distinctiveness of the Mahabharata. They did so in a beautiful and attractive manner. After hearing the story Taneshah wanted them to write a fresh epic in which he would figure as Dharmaraja, the eldest of the Pandavas, all the ministers whom he liked would figure as the other Pandavas and all his enemies would figure as the Kauravas. In other words, he asked them to write a Taneshah Bharata. These poets were not inclined to produce an epic of this kind and were discussing among themselves as to how they could tackle the situation. Amongst them a clever poet by name Tenali Ramakrishna came forward and said that he would undertake preparing this book. He wanted to teach a good lesson to the Taneshah. The Taneshah then asked him to prepare the text in a week's time. The week was coming to a close and Ramakrishna had not even started writing and the other poets were afraid that the Taneshah would punish them. By the end of the agreed period, Ramakrishna took a few pieces of paper and went to the Taneshah who in turn had invited many friends to listen to this great text. Taneshah asked Ramakrishna if the Bharata was completed. Ramakrishna said that it was nearly complete but that there were one or two minor doubts which required clarification from the Taneshah. Then the Taneshah asked him what these doubts were so that he could clarify them. Ramakrishna replied that he had some hesitation to raise these doubts in public and he would wish to do so when both of them were alone. Taneshah and Ramakrishna went in side and Ramakrishna said that he had a doubt as to who would fit in the role of Draupadi. Since Draupadi was wife to all the five Pandavas, the person in this role would have to be wife for the five Pandavas in the story. This means that Taneshah's wife would be a wife to the ministers as well. Ramakrishna asked Taneshah if he would agree to give this role to his wife. This was not at all liked by the Taneshah and he told Ramakrishna that there was no need to write such a Bharata and asked him to clear out after giving him suitable gifts. Thus we see here that the Taneshah wanted to have the reputation of the Pandavas but he did not want to accept the sacred terms under which the five Pandavas took Draupadi as their wife. Today, if we want to establish the nobility of our culture, we should realise and accept as a fact that the basis for it is respect for morality and truth. We should follow the path of morality and truth. If we want to have the reputation alone but not follow the path followed by our ancestors, we will only be doing what the Taneshah wanted to do. This will be leading an artificial life. We should not hanker after getting a name and cheap popularity. We should look to the fulfilment of life.

SABARI'S SADHANA

Sabari had a very tender, compassionate heart. How she came to Matanga Rishi and stayed at his hermitage is a very interesting story. Her marriage was arranged by her parents, and as was the custom among the Adivasis a goat was to be offered to the tribal Goddess, on the night previous to the ceremony, in order to win the Grace for the couple. When Sabari came to know about this slaughter, she wept, and fell at the feet of her parents, praying them to save the goat. She asked, "How can our married life be happy, when the dying bleat of this goat is the prologue?" But, the father pushed her aside and proceeded with the cruel rite. That night Sabari stole out of that den of torture, and hid herself in the depths of the jungle that was not far off.

When day dawned, her parents as well as the groom's party were plunged in grief and anxiety; they combed the area, even where she was lying low amidst the thick bushes, and they went back, saying among themselves, "She could not have gone to the hermitage, for no women would be given asylum there". She heard these words and so, she concluded that the hermitage was the safest place for her. She felt that some monk will take pity on her, and not send her back. Matanga espied her and gave her permission to be in his habitation. He told her that God in the form of Sri Rama was coming to the hermitage some day, since he has been exiled into the forests for 14 years and He is eager to save the monks and seekers, doing Tapas in the forests, from the ravages of the demonic enemies of peace! Rama, he said, was proceeding from one region to another, with His consort Sita and His brother, Lakshmana.

From that day Sabari had no other thought than of Rama, no other desire than the desire to have the Darsan of Rama, the chance to touch His Feet and the opportunity to speak with Him. Her heart was saturated with the Ramarasa, the sweetness of the Rama principle. She had no other Japam or Dhyana or spiritual exercise. She spent her time, preparing for the visit of Rama to the hermitage; just as she cleaned the paths, she cleaned her heart, too. Pebbles and thorns disappeared from both through her efforts. She walked through the undergrowth and removed overhanging creepers and briars, for she imagined Rama would not have combed His hair and it might get caught. She broke the lumps of earth, for she feared the tender soles of Sita will be hurt when she walks over them. She gathered fruits and tubers from the jungle trees and plants kept them by every day, for no one knew when Rama will arrive! And, she took no risks. She tasted every fruit, whether it was bitter, sour or sweet, so that Rama could eat the best. She smoothed the surface of all stones that lay by the side of the tracks in the jungle for, she expected Rama, Lakshmana or Sita to sit upon any one of them when they got tired of walking. She hoped that one of them would rest a while on one of the rocks she had polished with great care. Thus her heart became Ramahridaya!

Sabari was so immersed in Rama that the ascetics lost all awareness of her sex; they allowed her to remain in the hermitage, after Matanga related to them her high level of Sadhana. Matanga also left this body and gave up his hermitage to Sabari, saying, you alone deserve to be here when Rama arrives!

The Sadhana that Sabari did to earn the bliss of serving Rama, you can do, when you serve Sai Rama in the poor. By this service, you realise the self as Rama.

THE WORLD CONFERENCE OF ANIMALS

Man is the noblest of all animals, the final product of untold ages of progressive evolution; but he is not consciously striving to live up to his heritage. The beasts held world conference, to confabulate on the authenticity of man's claim to be the acme of creation and the monarch of all that walks the earth. The Lion presided over the deliberations. The tiger questioned the claims of man; the leopard seconded the resolution of emphatic protest. It made a devastating speech, condemning man, "He is a standing disgrace to animals everywhere. He manufactures and drinks merrily fatal poisons and is proud of his utter foolishness. He cheats his own kind and spends all his energies and resources in devising diabolic weapons to wipe out his sisters and brothers; he prods horses and dogs to run in desperate haste and gambles his earnings away, while they gallop long the track; he is cruel, greedy, immoral, insatiable and unashamed. He sets a bad example to the animal world. Though endowed with superior emotions and intelligence, his behaviour is disgusting and demeaning", he said. "We do not know if and where we will get our next meal ; we have no sure place of rest. We have nothing to wrap round ourselves, expect the skin. But, yet the least of us is a far worthier child of God than this monster called man" he concluded.

The fox rose and added," We have a season when we mate, but man, I am ashamed to say, has broken all regulations and cares for no restrain. He is a law unto himself and disaster to the rest.

The Lion rose, to sum up the arguments. He agreed with the general trend of the tirade man, provoked by his undeserved claim to supremacy. But, he refused to tar all with the same brush. He distinguished between men who are bestial and worse, and men who have transcended their bestial past by the proper use of the special gifts of discrimination and detachment. The latter, he said, ought to be received by all beasts as Masters, while the former deserved severe reprisals and condemnation.

SEEK THE POINT OF VIEW OF GOD

Four friends once started dealing in cotton. They had a godown for the storage of the bales ; finding that the cotton seeds attracted rats to the godown , a cat was introduced by them to scare the rodents throng. They tied jingles to her feet and since they loved it much, the jingles were of gold ! Once, when the cat jumped from the top of the pile of bales, it started limping on one foot. So they applied some balm and tied along strip of bandage round the injured foot. The bandage got loose and the cat, unaware of the long narrow cloth that was trailing behind her, sat near the fireplace ,and when the cloth began to burn she ran helter-skelter and fled into godown itself , where the entire stock of cotton was reduced to ashes in a trice. The four friends had assigned to themselves each. One of the feet of the joint cat and the injured foot belonged to one of them; so the other three charged him with the damages which they claimed from him.

The matter went to court and after hearing arguments on both sides, the judge said, "The injured leg has no responsibility, for it was taken into the godown with the trail of fire by the three healthy feet. So, damages have to be paid by the owners of the healthy feet to the owner of the limping foot ". What may thus appear correct at first sight, might prove wrong on second thoughts. There is a correctness from the worldly point of view and a correctness, from God's. Find out what the point of view of God would be, by association with godly men; they can give you proper advice. You must seek and not avoid good men.

ATMA TATWA IS ONE AND THE SAME IN ALL

There was a guru with a large number of disciples and the guru was telling them some good things. One day, when the lesson was going on, the teacher told the disciples that while they are engaged in pooja and meditation, no matter what obstacles come their way, they must take care to see that their meditation is not disturbed. The disciples had great faith in the guru. There were also some disciples who were staying in the ashram itself. On birthday of guru, one disciple decided to offer special prayers to the guru by repeating the 108 names of the Lord. The disciple collected a photograph, 108 flowers and wanted to perform the pooja in the traditional manner. One other disciple invited the guru and took him to his house. The guru while going told this other disciple, who wanted to do the worship at the ashram itself, to be careful and asked him to keep the door closed. The day was very hot and the guru neither had slippers for his feet nor did he have sufficient hair on his head to protect him from the sun. When the guru came to the ashram and wanted the door to be opened, the disciple inside was engaged in offering pooja. The guru knocked at the door and asked the disciple to open the door. The disciple replied that he was engaged in pooja and that the guru must wait till the pooja was over, as the pooja was not to be interrupted. Today ninety nine out of hundred people are like this disciple. They only worship the photograph of the person whose grace they long for, and continue to do so even when the latter is knocking at the very door of the worshipper.

THE ONE BASIS AND DIFFERENT CONTAINERS

When a guru was sitting and teaching his disciples, one day he said :Guru Brahma, Sishya Brahma, Sarvam Brahma. Thus the guru was implying that everything in the universe was Brahman. Every day, one disciple was accustomed to greet the guru respectfully on his arrival, but after this particular event, he did not do so and he never got up from his seat. The guru questioned him on this strange behaviour and the disciple replied that the previous day, the Guru had said that everything was Brahman and therefore there was no difference between them.

Then the teacher felt that what he said came back to him as a boomerang and he wanted to teach the student a good lesson. He went to the board and wrote "Guru Brahma" as two different words and wrote "Sishya Brahma", and "Sarvam Brahman ".When you look at these three, though Brahma is occurring as the same in all three, the Guru, Sishya and Sarvam are different. Only when these three words also become one, you can say that all are one .Thus, until you are able to experience this oneness of all in practice, the student will remain a student and a teacher will remain a teacher and there is no escape from the need for the student having to respect the teacher. The basis is one but the container are different .

THE RIGHT PATH TO LIBERATION

While devoting your life to worldly pleasures and ideas it is not possible for you to realise God.

There is a story of a king, who used to ask all people who came to his kingdom, to tell him the correct path for realisation. Each one, basing himself either on some standard text or on what elders told him, used to say that a particular path was the right one for liberation. While this was going on, a servant close to the King was listening to the many descriptions that were being given of the right path for liberation. He found that the king was listening continuously to various methods of attaining moksha but he was not putting any one of them into practice. With the intention of teaching the king a good lesson, one day when the king was sitting and taking to many people in the central hall, the servant came from out side shouting loudly. The king then got up and asked the servant what he was shouting for. The servant replied with some anxiety in his face that all the palace camels were climbing up to the top of the terrace. The King asked how the camels can climb to the terrace. The servant then said that if the King , steeped in luxury, can aspire to climb the path of spirituality and attain liberation and moksha, there need be no surprise at the camels climbing to the terrace, and running off.

EVERY ACT OF THE LORD HAS A SIGNIFICANCE

Arjuna's pride was humbled during the war in an interesting manner by Krishna. About the end of the war, one evening, Arjuna felt proud that Krishna was his charioteer and his 'servant'. He felt that as master, he should get down from the chariot after Krishna and not before Him. So, that day he asked that Krishna should get down first. But,Krishna was adament : Arjuna must come down first , he said. After wasting a long time, pleading protesting and praying, Arjuna got down, very unwillingly, swallowing his pride. Krishna then came down, and, immediately the chariot went up in flames! Krishna explained the reason. The incendiary arrows and missiles that had stuck on the chariot were powerless so long as He was on it; when his presence was no longer there, they set the chariot on fire. Thus, Krishna showed that every act and word of the Lord had significance and a purpose, which mortals cannot gauge. Egoism is a tough enemy and it requires constant vigilance to conquer it.

HUNUMAN'S DEVOTION

After the coronation, one day, Sita and the three brothers of Rama met and planned to exclude Hanuman from seva of Rama and wanted that all the various services for Rama should be divided only among themselves. They felt that Hanuman had enough chances already. So, they drew up a list, as exhaustive as they could remember, of the services from dawn till dusk, down to the smallest minutiae and assigned each item to one among themselves. They presented the list of item and assignees to the Lord, while Hanuman was present. Rama heard about the new procedure, read the list and gave His approval, with a smile. He told Hanuman that all the tasks had been assigned to others and that he could now take rest. Hanuman prayed that the list might be read and when it was done, he noticed an omission - the task of 'snapping finger when one yawns'. Of course, being an emperor, Rama should not be allowed to do it himself. It has to be done by a servant, he pleaded. Rama agreed to allot that task to Hanuman!

It was a great piece of good luck for Hanuman, for it entailed Hanuman's constant attendance to his Master, for how could anyone predict when the yawn could come? And, he had to be looking on that heart charming face all the time, to be ready with the snap, as soon as one yawn was on! He would not be away a for a minute nor could he relax for a moment. You must be happy that the seva of the Lord keeps you always in His presence and ever vigilant to carry out His behests.

KARNA :THE GREAT GIVER

There is fine story about Karna. He was applying oil to his head, preliminary to his bath, from a jewelled cup. Karna had taken the oil in his right hand and rubbed it well into his hair, when Krishna appeared and Karna rose to serve Him. He had come to demand the cup from him as a gift ! 'I am surprised that You, the Master of universe, have a desire for this paltry thing but who am I to ask you questions? Here is the cup, I gift it to you', he said and placed it in the Lords right hand with his left hand. Krishna took him to task for that error in dharma, offering a gift with the left hand. But Karna said, "Pardon me, O Lord! My right hand is smeared with oil; I am afraid, that if I take time to wash the hand and make it fit to give the cup, my wayward mind which now had agreed to the gift, might discover some argument not to accede to your request; I might therefore be deprived of the unique good fortune, by fickle mind with which I am burdened. This is the reason why I acted immediately and passed it on to you, regardless of the breach of a rule of etiquette; please sympathise with me and pardon me", Karna pleaded. Karna knew that the mind is unsteady. But, as Krishna advised Arjuna, it can be tamed by detachment and discipline.

VAIRAGYA - THE STORY OF MOHAJITH

Bhakti and the attitude of Saranaagathi that is its final fruit, will give you great courage to meet any emergency; such courage is What is Vairagya. The story of Mohajith is a good example of this highest type of Vairagya. Mohajith, the Prince, went to a Sage in the forest and sought guidance in spiritual path. The sage asked whether he had conquered Moha as his name indicated. The Prince said that not only he, but every one in his kingdom had ! So the sage started to test the truth of this claim. He took the Prince's robe, soaked them in blood and hastened to the Palace Gate with the gruesome story of the murder of the Prince by some ruffians in the jungle. The maid whom he met refused to hurry with the news to the Royal apartments because she said," He was born, he died; what is the urgency of this news that I should interrupt my regular routine and run to the King and Queen?" When at last he got an audience and was able to communicate the sad news to the father, he sat unruffled, whispering to himself," The bird flew off the tree on which it had alighted to take rest." The Rani too was unmoved.

She told the sage that this Earth is a caravanserai, where men come and stay for the night and when dawn breaks, one by one, they tramp their different ways. Kith and Kin are the words we use for the attachment to the travellers cultivated in the caravanserai during the short term of acquaintance. The wife of the "Dead" Prince was also unaffected; she said, "Husband and wife are like two pieces of wood drifting down a flooded river; they float near each other for some time and when some current comes between, they part; each must move on to the sea at its own rate and its own time. There is no need to grieve over the parting of the two; it is in the very nature of Nature that it should be so." The sage was overjoyed to see this steady and sincere Vairagya in the rulers and the ruled. He came back to the forest and told the Prince that while he was away, a hostile army had invaded his kingdom and slain the entire royal family and captured his kingdom and enslaved his subjects. He took the news calmly and said, "All this is but a bubble, impermanent, flimsy. Let it go the way of the bubble. Guide me to reach the Infinite, the Imperishable."

NEVER JUDGE ANOTHER'S DEVOTION

There is a widely prevalent habit now of judging other and labelling them as Bhakthas or Nastikas. What do you know, what can you know of the inner working of another's mind? There was once a queen who was a great devotee of Rama; she felt so sad that her husband, The Raja, never uttered the name of Rama and had no Bhakthi. She had vowed that the first occasion on which she got evidence of his Bhakthi or at least respect for Ramanama, she would conduct Puja on a lavish scale. Then, one night, while asleep, the Raja uttered the name of Rama thrice plaintively and prayer fully. She heard the Namasmarana and was so happy at the discovery of her husband's devotion to Rama; she ordered general rejoicing throughout the kingdom and the feeding of the poor. The Raja did not know the reason for the celebration for he was only told that it was an order of the Rani, which the officers carried out. Similarly, a husband may not be aware of the excellence of a wife's spiritual attainments. There is the case of a couple who were proceeding through thick jungle on pilgrimage to an inaccessible shrine. The husband saw on the footpath a precious stone, shining brilliantly when the sun's rays fell upon it from between the leaves. He hastily threw some sand over it with a movement of his foot so that his wife may not be tempted to pick it up and become a slave to the tinsel. The wife saw the gesture and chided the husband for still retaining in his mind a distinction between sand and diamond. For her, both were the same.

The Raja who spoke in his sleep the sacred name of Rama felt very sorry, according to the story that he let Ramanama out of his mouth, for he believed that no one should know of his 'love' for Rama. There are many who will not shout about their Guru or their favourite

Nama and Rupa but whether you declare them to others or not, keep them ever in your consciousness. Ramanama or any other name must be as constant as breathing. For this, practice is essential. A person once told Dr. Johnson, the famous English thinker, that he could seldom get time to recite the Name of God, what with the hundreds of things he had to do from morning till nightfall and even far into the night. Dr. Johnson replied with another question. He asked how millions of people found space to live upon the face of the earth, which is two thirds water and rest is too full of mountains, deserts, forests, icy regions, riverbeds, marshes and similar impossible areas. The questioner said that man somehow struggled to find living space. So too, said Dr.Johnson, man must somehow find a few minutes a day for prayer to the Lord.

GOD ON YOUR SIDE- WORLD IN YOUR HOLD

You may have accumulated riches, acquired deep scholarship and achieved health and strength. But, unless you have gained, in addition, a vision of the Supreme Sovereign, and an aspiration to be ever in the ecstasy of that vision, all that has been garnered by you is mere lumber. India has a great epic, the Mahabharata, which describes a war between the Kauravas and Pandavas. The Kauravas had superior financial and military resources. They approached Krishna, the incarnation of the Lord, for help; but, they were content to receive from Him a large army and huge quantity of hardware. The Pandavas sought from Him only His grace! The Lord agreed, He came to their side, alone and unarmed! He held just a whip and drove the horses of Arjuna's chariot! That was all that was needed for victory. The Kauravas were defeated to the utter most; the Pandavas won the empire and eternal fame.

If God is on your side, you have the world in your hold. This is the lesson driven home by the Hindu scriptures. "Give up all bonds of right and duty; surrender unreservedly to Me! I shall guard you from sin and liberate you from that sad cycle of 'entrances' and 'exits' on the stage of life. You can remain ever in your own Reality of Eternal Calm", the Lord has assured.

DHARMARAJA'S GRIEF OVER KARNA'S DEATH

Karna, the eldest born of the Pandavas, did not know that he was the brother of the other five. Nor did the five brothers know this fact. As a consequence of this ignorance, Karna was saturated with hatred towards the five; he longed to destroy them; he prepared himself for battle against them, with unabated vigour. The five younger brothers too, planned to destroy him and behaved towards him as if he were their deadly enemy. When Dharmaraja, the eldest of the five, came to know after the death of Karna, which they effected successfully - that Karna was his brother, his agony knew no bounds; he was disconsolate and was torn by despair. If only he had known the truth, all that grief could have been avoided, isn't it? So too, until you know that all are altars where the same God is installed, all are moved and motivated by the Grace of the self-same God, you are afflicted by hate and pride; once you know it and experience it, you are full of love and reverence to all. The barbarous remedy of war will be given up when basic brotherhood is felt in the deepest core of man.

KRISHNA IS THE VISUALISATION OF THE ATMA

The Krishna whose advent you should celebrate is not the cowherd boy who charmed the village folk with His flute, but, the Krishna, the indefinable, inscrutable, Divine principle that is born in the naval of the body (Mathura) as the product of the Energy (Devaki), that is then transported to the Mouth (Gokulam) and fostered by the Tongue (Yashoda) as its source of sweetness. Krishna is the visualisation of the Atma, that the repetition of the name grants; the Vision that was gained by Yasoda. You must foster that Krishna on your tongue; when he dances on it the poison of the tongue will be rejected completely, without harming anyone, as happened when as child he danced on the hoods of the serpent Kalinga.

Yasoda traces Krishna to the place He hides in, by the footprints He leaves, when He has broken the curds pot, which she was churning. This is a symbolic story to illustrate how the lord brakes our identification with body and leads us on to Himself, by signs and signals that He provides all round us. These signs are ever present in the nature around each one of us, in the beauty of the rising sun, the ecstasy of the rainbow, the melody of the birds, the lotus-spangled surface of lakes, the silence of snow-crowned peaks-in fact, since God is rasa, sweetness, ecstasy, all nature, which is but Himself in action is sweet and ecstatic. With or without form, it is Ananda. Welcome it into the heart as Rama - He who is joy and grants joy - or as Krishna - He who draws you by means of the joy He imparts - and, live all your moments with it, offering it your dhyana, your pooja, your japa. That will open the doors of jnana and of liberation. This is the mark of the wise, while those who are otherwise wander in the wilderness, filling their moments with meaningless trifles, toys and geegaws.

NARADA BHAKTHI SUTRAS

Narada asked Vishnu once : "The rishis or sages who had attained the purest wisdom relating to the universal Atma could not win your grace; but the illiterate milkmaids of Gokul who were charmed by Your beauty, Your sport, Your music, Your prattle, Your sweetness, Your inscrutable novelty-they won your grace. How did this happen?" But, Narada himself came to know later that the gopis had Krishna (The Lord) as the very breath of their lives, as the very sight of their eyes, the very sound of their ears, the very taste of their tongues, the very touch of their skin. While tending the cows and calves, attending to their husbands and their children, doing the thousand and one chores of worldly life, they lived in Krishna, with Krishna, and by means of Krishna only; *Sarvada Sarva Kaleshu Hari Chintanam.* Under all conditions, at all times, in all places, their minds dwelt on Hari (Krishna-the Lord). How then can God deny them grace?

When Narada went to Gokul and called the gopis to gather around him so that they can listen to his teachings about the attainment of jnana, the gopis gave no heed; they said, they did not like to waste precious minutes. "The hours of day and night are not enough for us to dwell on the name of the Lord. We do not require your verbal acrobatics to convince us that God is Satchitananda swarupa; we know, we feel, we experience the bliss every moment". It was after this revelation of the supremacy of Bhakthi that Narada composed the Bhakthi Sutras, which have become the guiding lamps for aspirants.

PLAYING MARBLES WITH THE NAME OF GOD

There was once a boy, who picked up a precious gem, bright and round, and used it for playing marbles on the road, with his comrades. A merchant dealing in precious stones chanced to pass along that road, and his discerning eye fell on the gem. He approached the boy, took him aside and offered to pay him fifty rupees in exchange. If the boy could know the value of fifty rupees he would have known the value of the gem! He went to his mother and told her that a stranger had tempted him with fifty rupees in return for the marble he played with. She was surprised that it was so costly and she said, "Do not go out of the compound with it; play in the garden with your friend". When the value was revealed, limits were set.

The merchant had no sleep that night; he was planning to secure the gem from those simple folk, so that he could sell it at a huge profit to some millionaire or maharaja. He discovered the house of the boy and moved up and down that road hoping see the boy . When he saw the boy play with it as it was as cheap as a marble, his heart was wrung in agony. The boy threw it on the floor; his mother emerged just at the moment from the inner apartments and it struck her foot and fell under a bush. He spoke to the boy asking for the gem in exchange for a hundred rupees, and again, for five hundred rupees ! The son ran into the house in tears, complaining about the stranger who would not let him alone. The mother came out into the garden and begged the merchant to go away.

The merchant grasped away the chance ; he told the mother that he was ready to give even a thousand rupees on the spot, if the marble was placed in his hand !On hearing this, she forbade the child to play with it outside the house ;he could play only within the rooms. The merchant could not be shooed off like that; he appeared the next day in front of the house; he held out ten thousand rupees as his offer for the marble;

the mother refused to part with it but kept it now in an iron safe, under lock and key! When the merchant came the next day with fifty thousand rupees she took it to a bank and deposited it in their safety vaults. You are also playing marbles with the name of God, unaware of its value. Once you realise its worth, you will keep it in your heart of hearts as the most precious treasure. Know that the name is the key to success in your search for consolation, confidence, courage, illumination and liberation.

CHAITANYA - INCARNATION OF KRISHNA

Chaitanya gave indications of his being an incarnation, to His mother, as a child. Chaitanya was then a baby crawling on all fours. His mother had a guest in the house, an old orthodox Brahmin, who was cooking his own lunch from the provisions given by her. He desired that the food to be ceremonially pure, uncontaminated by the touch of other hands. He offered to God the food he proposed to eat; that was his vow. It was rather late when the offering was ready. Just when he sat before the idol of Krishna for worship, the child toddled forward and dipped his fingers in the vessel of food thus making it 'impure' as an offering to God. So, provisions were given again, food was cooked again, and very late in the day, the worship resumed. This time, too, the child crawled in from somewhere and contaminated the sacred food ! It repeated the mischief a third time. The mother dragged the child away and threatened to thrash the prank out of its head. But the child asked the mother quite innocently, "He is calling on me to eat it, but, when I go near it he gets angry." Thus did he reveal that He was Krishna again.

THE GREATER GRIEF SCOURS OFF THE SMALLER

When Dasaratha the Emperor died, there was no one at hand to perform the obsequies and so, they sent words to the younger sons, Bharata and Satrughna, who had left for kinsman's capital. They were not informed of the death, and when they came and saw the body, they were too shocked at the inert silence of their dear father, that they ran to Kausalya, the queen, their step mother. She burst into tears when the two boys ran into her apartments. They were shocked at this and inquired why. It was then that she broke the sad news of the death of their father. Bharata was plunged in grief at this tragedy; he wept aloud beating his breast. It was inconsolable agony. Then amidst the distress he said, "Mother, how unfortunate I am. I had no chance to nurse him in his illness, during his last days. Alas! Dear brother, you too lost the precious chance of service", he said patting Satrughna on the head. After some moments, he continued, "Mother, how fortunate are Rama and Lakshmana. They were with him. They nursed him and ran on little errands for him. They were with him when he breathed his last. Since we were far away, did father leave any command for us? What was his last wish regarding us? Did he remember us, ask that we should be sent for?" Kausalya said, "Son, he had only one word on his lips, one form before his eye; that word was Rama, that form was Rama". Bharatha looked surprised. He asked, "How is it that he uttered the name and craved for the form of Rama, who was by his bedside, and did not yearn for me who was far away? O, how unlucky I am? I have lost the affection of my dear father." Kausalya replied, "Well, if Rama had been by his side or near him, he would not have passed away". Bharatha ejaculated, "Mother, where had Rama gone? Why was he away? Where is he now?

Did he go a-hunting to the forest? Was he on a pleasure trip on the Sarayu?" The mother said, "No, no. He has gone into the forest for fourteen years". Bharatha could bear it no longer. "Alas, what an outrageous tragedy, this? What crime, what sin did Rama commit to deserve this exile? Why had he to go?" " Your mother wished that he should go, and so he went" said the queen.

When Bharatha heard this, the grief that he sustained on hearing the death of his father paled, and the grief that arose at his mother sending Rama into exile for fourteen years supervened overwhelming all else. The grater grief scours off the smaller .

COMPASSION IS A SIGN OF THE GREAT

Once when Samartha Ramdas was moving about the country side with his disciples, those behind him seeing a fine field of juicy sugar cane, entered it and started pulling out the cane, with great relish. The owner of the field naturally enraged at their behaviour and at the loss to which they were subjecting him, fell upon them with a stout cane. The Master was sorry that his disciples broke discipline so objectionably drawn by the desire of the tongue for the sweet juice. Next day they reached Emperor Sivaji's place, where a great welcome awaited the Guru and his followers. Sivaji offered to attend personally to the Guru during his ceremonial bath; When Ramadas undressed, Sivaji was shocked to find broad red marks, indicating that he had been beaten ! Such was the sensitive sympathy of the great saint, that he received on his back the blows meant for his pupils. Sivaji sent for the owner of the field of cane; and, when he stood shivering in fear before the Emperor and his Guru, Ramadas was requested by Sivaji to inflict on him any punishment he liked. But, Ramadas accepted the fact that wrong was committed by his disciples and blessed the farmer, granting him a boon that his lands would be tax free forever.

REWARD FOR SINCERE YEARNING

There was a Sultan once, ruling over the region of Mathura, Brindavan and other places, on the Yamuna. During his reign the Emperor of Vijayanagar came on pilgrimage and stayed at Brindavan for some days, where he paid homage to Krishna in the temple. The Sultan argued that he must have come so only to pay respects to someone greater than himself. He was determined to see that one, come what may. So late one night he went and called out before the closed doors of the temple, "Who is inside? " He heard a voice which gave the reply, "Govind Maharaj and Radha Rani ". The Sultan was now sure that there were two persons living inside, a Super - Emperor and His Super-Empress. He was filled with an agonising yearning to see the distinguished occupants of the temple. He waited outside the door, without food or drink for three full days. He was overcome with hunger and thrust; but he did not stir, for he was afraid the Imperial Couple may emerge any moment and he might miss the Darsan.

That night, when the town was asleep, just before midnight Govind Maharaj and Radha Rani emerged from the temple. They signed to him to follow them. They were magnificently dressed and had elaborately bejewelled headgears, necklaces, wristlets and ornaments for the hands and feet. They moved on until they reached the banks of the Yamuna, where thousands of gopas and gopis were gathered to welcome them. There was music and dance in the bright moon light, heavenly joy shown on every face. At 4 A.M.. they returned to the temple and before they passed through the closed door, they gave into his hands the Kankanas they wore on their wrists, for safe keeping. Before he could say anything, they had gone.

A party of priests came along at that time, and seeing him, asked him, why he was standing there and what he had in his hands. They had come to open the locks of the outer and inner doors and inaugurate the ceremonials of the day, with Suprabhatam and Nagarasamkirtan. (Awakening Hymn and Moving Choirs) The Sultan said, "Govind Maharaj and Radha Rani have just gone in; I saw them at the Yamuna Bank from midnight till a few minutes ago. They gave me these kankanas for safekeeping. I don't know why." They surmised he was a thief who, caught in the act, was spinning a yarn and so bound him and beat him. Only the idol of Krishna had no gold kankanas ! Now they were convinced that the man outside was a great Bhaktha, who had the unique vision of the Lord. They honoured him and craved pardon for the wrong perpetrated in ignorance. Such is the reward for sincere yearning; unlimited ananda can be earned through implicit faith in God.

THE MOST AMAZING THING ON EARTH

When once Brahma asked the sage Narada, what was the most amazing thing he noticed on earth, Narada replied, "The most amazing thing I saw was this- the dying are weeping over the dead". Those who are themselves nearing death are weeping over those who have died , as if their weeping has any effect, either to revive the dead or prevent their own death ! Brahma asked him to tell another. Narada said, "Another sequence is : Everyone fears the consequence of sin, but goes on sinning nevertheless ! Everyone craves for the consequence of punya (meritorious acts), but everyone is reluctant to do any meritorious act!"

THE BEST FRIEND IN LIFE

Friendship rampant these days can be illustrated by a story. A person had three friends. He had taken to several bad ways and consequently had to face a court case. He went to a friend and asked for help. The friend blankly told him that he would not like to associate himself with the crime committed by him. He refused to give evidence to rescue him. The second friend, when approached, told him that he would only go up to the court but would not be a witness in a witness box. Thereafter he approached the third friend for help. He immediately responded and said, "Yes, your troubles are mine, my troubles are yours and I shall help you in whatever manner you wish me to help." It is quite clear that amongst these three the third is the best kind of friend. For your life also we have such friends. At the time of death, one has to leave behind all that one owns. Wealth and status do not accompany you. Your friends and relations may come to the burial ground to bury or cremate the body, and thereafter all will return home. Only the good and bad acts that you have performed in your life will accompany you. Your next birth will be carved out according to your deeds in this life. In order to remain good, you must cultivate respect for truth which is permanent, whereas everything else including your body is subject to change, decay and death.

WORLDLY PLEASURES ARE LIKE A SERPENT'S GRIP

One person came to Me about 20 years ago and prayed that he should meet with success in his examination and a high first class. I told him that there will have to be effort and the result will be according to

God's will. I gave him my blessings and sent him away. He did secure a high first class and came to Me gain after passing his examination and asked for My blessings so that he may get a job. He did get a job within a month. He came to me after a few months. He said he got a job, that he was happy, and he also said he wanted to marry a typist girl in his own office. I told him that if it is agreeable to his father and mother, he may do so but they may not like it. He was not inclined to listen to me. He said even if it is transgressing the wishes of his parents, he was determined to marry that girl. He in fact suggested that he would give up his life, if this marriage was not possible. I told him that he must convince his parents before he entering into such an alliance. He brought a lot of pressure on his parents and they, finding no other alternative, agreed to the marriage. The marriage was over and after a year, both of them came to Me again and said they wanted a son. After the birth of a son his expenses multiplied, his wife gave up the job, and he came to Me desiring a promotion. By his good luck he got a promotion. Although he was somewhat foolish in regard to worldly matters, he had great faith in regard to matters relating to Swamy. I gave him my blessings and he got a promotion. He did not turn up thereafter for over five years. He was quite happy and in the next five years, they had four children. He came again to Me after five years and said that he was fed up with the family, he cannot bear the burden of the family and was looking for relief from all the mess. He said that he wanted a small job in the ashram itself and said that his family has now got hold over him like a big serpent. I asked him if the serpent caught him on its own or whether he let the serpent come to him and catch him.

SOUND IS SACRED

One teacher, having about 10 students, was teaching them some good things. To such an ashram came one who had some position and power. This teacher did not go to the door to welcome and receive him. This man who came there, because he had some position and authority, felt somewhat hurt and he went right into the class and asked the teacher, "Why is it you did not care for me? You have not come and received me. What are you doing ?" The teacher said, "I am busy teaching the children some good things." The person who came in asked " Just because you are teaching some good things, are the hearts of these children going to be changed and become more sacred?" The teacher took some courage and said, "Yes, of course, there is every possibility of their mind changing by my teaching.' The intruder said, "No, I can not believe it.", and the teacher replied: 'When you can not believe it, it simply means you have no faith in it. Because of that, I cannot give up teaching some good things." Then this person, who felt somewhat important, started arguing and said there is no possibility of changing a mind merely by words. The teacher who was clever and who had known these things asked one of the youngest boys to stand up. In the hearing of the visitor, the teacher told the boy," Look here ! My dear boy! Just get hold of the neck of this visitor and throw him out of the door." Immediately on hearing these words, the visitor became completely excited and his eyes were red and he was very angry and he came to beat the teacher. Then the teacher asked, "Sir, What is the reason for your becoming so angry? We did not beat you, we did not throw you out, the only thing that has exited you to this stage of anger is the word which I conveyed to this young boy. You, who said that you do not believe in changing the mind by mere words, what is the reason why these mere words which I have uttered to this young boy have changed your mind so much that you are so excited? So it is very wrong to say that with mere words you cannot change with the mind. With mere words you can cause any excitement. With mere words you can cause any amount of affection. With mere words you can earn the grace of anyone else". So, if in this world you want to promote friendship, you can do so by using sweet words, by talking in a very sweet manner and by speaking about sacred things. On the other hand if you use harsh words, you are not going to promote friendship in this world.

BRAHMAN IS ALL PERVADING

In the Upanishads, we have the story of one individual who was a very learned man who was himself a guru. His name is Uddalaka. He had a son by name Swethaketu.This son Swethakethu made several attempts to get his education at the feet of his own father Uddalaka. But the father did not agree to such a procedure. The reason for this is, for a son who moves freely with his father, it is rather difficult for both himself and the father to deal with and abide by the right disciple- and- guru relationship. The son will always have the idea that the teacher is his father and the concept of father and son will persist. This is because of the affection that obtains between the father and son. Here you will also have the justification for calling the son a 'Kama putra', a son who was born out of affection. Where there is attachment, where there is affection and where there is a feeling of belonging to, then there will be lenience and it is not possible to impart education in its fullest measure and with the right discipline. Because Uddalaka understood and realised the situation that education cannot be complete and proper when there is a relationship of attachment, he sent his son Swetaketu to another guru and desired that his son be taught and given proper education.

Looking at this situation, Swetaketu being young and inexperienced, mistook and interpreted it to himself wrongly and got the feeling that perhaps his father is not quite learned and hence has no competence to teach him and hence he is being sent to another guru for studies. For some years Swetaketu stayed in the Guru's house and completed his education and came back to his father's house with some conceit of high learning. Noticing this, the father asked the son, "what is it that you have learnt? What are the various systems that you have learnt? Have you learnt about Brahman? Have you learnt that particular branch of education which if one has learnt, one need not have to learn anything else and will be knowing all ?" Such were the questions by the father. While the father was asking these questions, the son was behaving in a rather queer and funny way. He was still showing superior airs and conceit as if he was far more educated and learned than his father and that the latter would not understand at all if he started telling what he had learnt over those few years. The father could easily understand the false vanity and the immature state of his son. The son was trying to show off, replying to his father that God is like this, God is like that, and so on.

Uddalaka felt that his son will not be able to grasp anything at all if he tried to tell him the Truth about Brahman in words. He thought it better to teach him by example. So he brought a pot filled with water. He brought also some sugar in his hand and he showed the sugar to the son. After showing him the sugar, he put all that sugar into the water in the pot. Then he stirred the sugar till it was completely dissolved in the water and then looked at the son and asked him: "I brought the sugar with me and you have seen the sugar yourself. I have put it into the vessel. Can you tell me where in this vessel does that sugar lie now?" The son looked into the vessel and of course did not find any sugar remaining as such in the vessel. The father put a few drops of the contents of the vessel from the bottom on the tongue of the son and asked, "How do you find the taste? You can take a drop from anywhere within the vessel and taste it." The son had to agree that sugar was there now in every drop of the contents of the vessel and that it was present everywhere in that vessel. Then the father explained saying: "Just as you have now seen this sugar being present everywhere, so also Brahman assumes the form of a 'saguna' or who has attributes and comes into this world and resides in everything that you see around you in this world. It is possible to see Him separately with your eyes, it is not possible to get hold of Him separately with your hands, but it is only possible to recognize Him by experiencing Him in the state of the world. You cannot do anything more with your gross body than to experience Brahman who is omnipresent and all pervading". It is only after you have attained this rich experience that you will be in a position to talk of Advaita and give expression to the nature of God, His omnipresence etc. It is only after such an experience will you have any claim, right and authority to talk about the omnipresence of God. Otherwise, with mere book-knowledge, prattling like a parrot about God and His Omnipresence, as if you truly know all, is all untruth. Only after the non-dual experience of Divinity can you talk of Advaita or nondualism.

LEAVE EVERYTHING TO HIS WILL

Yearning leads to surrender, and surrender gives highest joy. Leave everything to His will, accept whatever happens wether pleasant or painful. There was a rich merchant once in Baghdad. He was leading a virtuous God-fearing life. He had a daughter whom he adored greatly, for she was the very embodiment of virtue. The father decided that he will give her in marriage only to a young man who was intimately bound with God, regardless of any other excellence or handicap. He searched for such a groom, in caravanserais, mosques and places where holy persons were likely to gather. One Friday he noticed in the mosque a fair young man, on his knees, even after all else had left, crying out to God most endearingly and with sincerity. He approached him and asked whether he would marry his daughter. He said "I am the poorest of the poor: I have a leaky roof over my head , and a gravel floor whereon I sit. Who will wed such a beggar? I shall marry if some one who would not object to my spiritual Sadhana, consents to share my poverty".

The merchant felt that he was the most eligible groom and the wedding was celebrated soon. His daughter came to the fakir's residence and started cleaning the floor. She was happy that her husband was of her own heart; she too was a pilgrim on the road to God, a practitioner of spiritual exercises. While sweeping the floor, she found in a corner a plate with a piece of bread on it. She asked him why it was kept there, and he replied, 'I kept it by, lest tomorrow, when I go my rounds, we may not get enough to eat'.

At this, the wife replied, 'I am ashamed of you. You have so little faith in Allah. He who gives us hunger, will He not give us bread, too? I shall not live with a person of this nature. You have no faith in god and His Compassion' she said, and left the fakir to himself.

GOD MAKES HIMSELF AWARE TO BEASTS AND BIRDS

There are people who bring forth your tears when they pass away; there are others who bring forth your tears, when they pass across your way ! They are to be avoided. God makes himself aware to beasts and birds, rather than man, who has strayed into the wilderness. Recently at Dharmavaram, a jutka full of men and luggage was being driven towards the railway station, the driver beating the horse mercilessly on the back and neck so that it may run fast. A bearded old man, fair and rosy in health, was passing that way. He accosted the driver and said, "Here! Don't hold the reins so tight. Leave them free, hold them loose! The horse will then run fast". The driver retorted, "You keep quite! I know my horse better". One of the men inside the jutka said, "Who do you think he is?" The driver said, "I don't care"! The driver then heard a voice (it was the horse that spoke). "He is Krishna, who drove the horses of Arjuna's chariot: He knows all about horses!" The driver thought that the voice belonged to some one among his fare. He replied looking into the jutka. "He may know all about Arjuna's horses; but what does he know about mine?"

THE GOPI'S MESSENGER

The Gopis felt that a bee can sympathise with their pangs of separation from Krishna, more than any human messenger. They asked the bee to intercede with the Lord, on their behalf. Pray to Him, to bear the garland of my adoration, one Gopi asked the bee. Another wanted it to ask Krishna to illumine the darkness of her heart. Radha asked it to pray to Krishna to make the desert sands of her heart sprout into green, so that His feet may tread thereon, light and soft.

YOU CANNOT PAINT THE WORLD GREEN

Before you experience the Divine in every being in the universe and in every cell and atom, you have to experience it in yourselves. Each act, word and thought must be charged with that awareness. There was a millionaire once who was bothered by two aches, one in his stomach and the other in his head! He was diagnosed and treated. He was examined and treated by galaxy of medical experts; he consumed heavy loads of drugs, and underwent centuries of injections. But the aches persisted with greater vigour than ever before! At last, a swami (monk) arrived at the scene of his agony. He spoke very kindly to him, and pronounced the fault to be in his eye! Set right the eye, and the head on top and the stomach below would both behave very sweetly! To improve the eye, concentrate on only one colour. Concentrate on green he suggested. Do not fall on red or yellow, or any other colour.

The millionaire got together a group of painters and purchased barrels of green colour and directed that every object on which his eye was likely to fall be painted thick green. Just as the ashtagraha calamity (the ominous astrological phenomenon of eight heavenly bodies reaching a straight line in space, which was sought to be avoided by superstitious persons through ceremonials of exorcism) resulted in a rich harvest for priests, the millionaire's malady resulted in a rich harvest for paint craftsmen. When the Swami came back to him after about ten days, the craftsmen ran towards him with a bucket of green paint for he wore a red gown! He wondered why, and got the answer that their master dare not cast his eye on any colour other than green, lest the aches may return! The Swami reprimanded the patient, and said that he had wasted lakhs of rupees as a result of his monumental stupidity. "If only you had purchased a pair of green spectacles, worth perhaps four rupees, you could have saved these walls and trees and pots and pans, chairs and sofas and also a pretty large share of fortune! You cannot paint the world green."

LAKSHMANA COUNSELS GUHA

The knowledge that you are the architect of your fortune and that you can, by steady effort, rebuild it or foster it, that you are every day laying on or pulling down the structure of your career, will be a great inspiration provided you welcome it. It was the first night of Rama, Lakshmana and Sita in the thick jungle into which they were exiled. Guha, the chieftain of the fishermen, who had rowed them across the Ganges was engaged in subdued conversation with Lakshmana, while Rama and Sita were sleeping on the river bank! Guru was sunk in sorrow, that the inheritor of the empire should be cast on the sands under the sky; he cursed the Queen and her wicked accomplices for contriving this heartbreaking tragedy. But, Lakshmana prayed that he halt his tirade. 'I too emitted fiery fury at the perpetrators of this tragedy. For, I did not then know the inner purpose of this chapter of Rama's history. He has come in this human form to destroy the evil brood of demons, and so, He has himself contrived this exile, to be free from imperial responsibilities until that aim is accomplished! What do we know, dear Guha, of the mysteries of God or even of man, who is but God in human attire? Or of any living being or non-living matter, for they are all the inscrutable Divine, appearing to our limited senses in the way they do. What their real nature is, how can we ever know, with these inefficient instruments of knowledge?"

KALIDASA'S BHAKTHI GREATER THAN HIS YUKTHI

Kalidasa in the court of Bhojaraja was insulted by the senior poets and scholars who were jealous of his attainments. He was poor and that was enough reason for them to look down upon him. When the tank is full the frogs sit round its bank and croak; when it is dry, no frog leaps by its side. The seniors spread scandals about Kalidasa and attempted to cast him out of court.

Kalidasa knew of only one person who was free from jealousy and pride and that was Kali, the Mother. So, he went to the Kali temple and prayed before the mother to assure him of high status among poets. After a longtime spent in intense prayer, Kalidasa heard a voice emanating from the shrine which extolled Dandi and Bhavabhuthi as great geniuses and scholars. There was not even a whisper about his attainments! So, he got hurt and even enraged; he gave vent to his ire in harsh words and insisted that she should declare the truth, however unpleasant. Then, the voice announced, "*Thwamevaham, thwamevaham, thwamevaham, na samsayah*" (you are Myself, you are Myself, you are Myself, without doubt). What greater status did Kalidasa need than this? That is the reply that every seeker will get, for that is his truth, his reality, his prize, his comsummation.

There are many stories which describe Kalidasa as a very resourceful poet who defeated the stratagems of his opponents by clever tricks; but his Bhakthi was much greater than his yukthi. I am reminded of the yukthi of a house holder when he heard at midnight the noise of his house being broken into by thieves. He guessed that they were within earshot and so, he asked his wife loud enough to be heard by the thieves, "why are you torturing me thus, asking me to bring back all your jewels that I have pledged with the Marwari? I know that all your gold has gone to him and you know that I have not even a rupee with me; let good times come; I shall certainly recover them and give you. But, now?"! You need not be told that the thieves left, to enter some other house that night; they left the house that had "no gold, not even a rupee".

BHARATHA'S ADORATION OF RAMA

The Rama principle is the Principle of Love that descended from Heaven, as the Gift of the Gods, as a result of the Great Sacrifice. Rama means Delight! Nothing delights more than one's own innate self, and so , Rama is also known as Atma Rama. How then could Bharatha agree to usurp the throne, of which Rama is the rightful heir? He and Satrughna were at the Kekaya Capital, when Rama was exiled and Dasaratha died heart broken at the separation. News was sent to him, and when he entered the palace, unaware of the double tragedy that had cast its gloom over the city, he sensed some calamity. Vasishta, the family preceptor, advised him to ascend the throne, for the empire was suffering an interregnum!

Bharatha appealed that he be allowed to go to " the God of my prayers, the Lord who receives the homage of my unceasing adoration". Vasishta told him that it was his father's command, and his preceptor's counsel that he sit enthroned as Ruler. Bharatha replied that the request was proof of the extreme hatred that the parents, the people, the preceptor and everyone in Ayodhya had towards him, for, had they loved him, they would not have pressed him to commit such a mean sin. Bharatha stood before Vasishta with folded palms;

he prayed, "Is it just, is it fair, that you should burden me with the sovereignty over a kingdom, which slew my father, widowed my mother, exiled my dearest brother whom I value more than my very breath to the demon-ridden jungle, with his dearly beloved queen and which finally brought indelible disgrace on my mother? My empire is the realm which Rama rules over, namely, my heart, which is too small to contain His glory." Bharatha's name itself signifies that he is saturated with love of Rama. (Bha-means, Bhagavan-the Lord, Rama; ratha-means, pleased by, happy over, attached to).

Let the Love for the Lord grow in you, as it did in Bharatha. Let that sense of adoration, which discarded even a throne, flourish in you. Then you can be of great use to your country, your culture, your society, your religion and your community. Or else, all this bother that you have undergone, to attend Sathsangh, to listen to spiritual discourses, study spiritual texts, etc. will be a colossal exercise in futility.

PRACTISE SELF-CONTROL WITH STEADY FAITH

Those who deny God are denying themselves and their glory. All have Love in their hearts, in some form or other, either towards the children or the poor or their work or goal. That Love is God, the spark of the Godly in them. They have Ananda however small or temporary and that is a spark of God and the Godly. They have santi, detachmennt, sympathy. All these are reflections of the Divine on the mirror of their minds. These are all mental excellences, revealed through an appreciation of the advantages of virtue. Santhi or calmness practised through helplessness, as in the case of the thief in the story of Tenali Ramakrishna, is no good. One thief exhibited great Santi and Sahana, calm fortitude!

Noticing that a thief had come into his garden at night and that he was hiding under a "snake-gourd bush" near the well, Ramakrishna called his wife to his presence. He asked her to bring a rope and bucket so that he may draw water from the well. The wife drew the water and gave the bucket to him. The thief watched his movements and he crouched in the darkness, expecting that the man and his wife would go into house soon. He planned that he should gain entry later and collect his loot without being caught. Meanwhile, Ramakrishna pretended that he had something in his throat. He poured the water into his mouth, gargled loud and spat underneath the "snakegourd bush" right where the thief was crouching! He got it right on his face, and that was Ramakrishna's intention too. The poor fellow could not run away, he could not protest, he was afraid to move; he showed perfect fortitude. But, do you call it a virtue? Do you appreciate him for it? He was motivated by fear, not faith. Such Santhi and Sahana are of no use at all. Practise self-control, with steady faith. Then it is a source of strength.

THE LORD CARES FOR THE FEELING BEHIND THE ACT

Abdullah was sleeping in a corner of a mosque in Mecca, when he was awakened by the conversation of two angels above his head. They were preparing a list of the Blessed and one angel was telling the other that a certain Mahbub of Sikandar City deserved to be ranked first, even though he has not come on pilgrimage to the Holy City. Hearing this, Abdullah went to Sikandar City and found out that he was a cobbler, repairing the shoes of people. He was famished and poor; for, his earnings barely sufficed to keep flesh and bone together. He had by severe sacrifice piled up a few coppers during the course of years; one day, he spent the entire treasure to prepare a special dish which he proposed to place before his enceinte wife as a surprise gift. When he was proceeding home with the gift he heard the cry of a starving beggar who seemed to be in the throes of extreme hunger. Mahbub could not proceed further; he gave the pot containing the costly delicacy to the man and sat by his side, enjoying the blossoming of satisfaction on his haggard face. The act gave him a place of honour in the register of the Blessed, a place which pilgrims to Mecca who had spent millions of Dinars in charity could not secure. The lord cares for the feeling behind the act, not the fanfare and the fuss.

GURU- THE LAST RESORT

An aspirant after spiritual realisation went off into a jungle and was plodding across the infested region, through the thick undergrowth, when he heard the angry roar of a lion: he climbed a tree to escape from the beast, but the lion saw him among the branches and roamed round and round the trunk in terrific rage. On the tree, he was attacked by a bear and so, he slid down the roots that descended from one of the branches of that banyan tree. Luckily, there were two roots hanging from the branch, so that he could hang on in midair clinging to them, one in each hand. Just then, he saw two rats, one white and the other black, which were gnawing at the base of the roots, endangering his life with every bite. When in this perilous state, a honeycomb which was full of sweet nectar situated on one of the top branches leaks a few drops which fell his way; so, the unfortunate man put out his tongue to catch a drop so that he may taste the delicious honey, But no drop reached his tongue. In despair and terror, he called on his Guru, "O Guruji, come and save me" .The Guru who was passing by heard his appeal; he sped to the rescue; he brought a bow and arrows and slew the lion and bear, frightened off the rats and saved the disciple from the fear of death. Then , he led the man to his own Ashram and taught him the path of liberation.

This is the story of every one of you. This world is the jungle in which you roam; fear is the lion, which drives you up the tree of Samsara, worldly activities; anxiety is the bear that terrifies you and dogs your steps in Samasara; so, you slide down into attachments and binding deeds, through the twin roots of hope and despair. The two rats are day and night which eat away the span of life. Meanwhile, you try to snatch a little joy from sweet drops of egoism and mine-feeling. Finding at last that the drops are trivial and out of reach, you shout in the agony of renunciation, calling on the guru; the guru appears, whether from within or without, and saves you from fear and anxiety.

FREEDOM FROM EGOISM - FIRST QUALIFICATION OF A BHAKTHA

Worry and grief there will always be, of one type or other-in the past, present and future; while walking, dreaming and sleeping. But place faith in the Lord and do your tasks as dedicated to Him and they will vanish. Narada one day boasted before Vishnu that no devotee could excel him; but this boast was against the very first qualification of a Bhaktha - freedom from egoism. So, Vishnu spoke of a ryot who was tilling his little plot of land as a greater devotee and recommended that Narada should visit him and learn the art of devotion from him! Narada felt very much humiliated and he proceeded to the village indicated in great chagrin. He found the ryot engrossed in his round of duties on the field and in the cattle shed and home and in spite of the most vigilant watch, he could not hear him speak the name of the lord more than thrice a day: once when he woke up from bed, another time when he took his midday meal and the last, when he retired for the night. Narada was naturally incensed that he was deemed inferior to this very poor specimen of a Bhaktha. He was always singing melodiously the leelas of the Lord and spreading everywhere the message of namasankirthana and there was a horny-handed son of soil who remembered the Lord just three times a day, whom Vishnu judged as superior to him. He hurried to heaven, his face flushed with anger and ignominy; but, Vishnu only laughed at his plight. He gave him a pot full to the brim with water and asked him to carry it on his head and go round a certain course with out spilling even a drop. Narada did so, but when asked how often he had remembered the Name of the Lord, he admitted that in his anxiety to walk without shaking the pot and spilling the water, he had forgotten the Name completely. Then Vishnu told him that the ryot who was carrying on his head more precious and more spillable burdens than a pot of water and who had to be careful not to bring harm to any of them, must perforce be admired for remembering the Lord at least three times a day.

Therefore it will be great gain if you remember the Lord with thankfulness at least thrice or even twice a day; that will give you great peace. Do not give up your worldly duties, but do them with the name of God on your lips, inviting the Grace of God on you.

DESIRE BINDS US

Those who catch monkeys prepare a pot with a small opening and fill it with some sweets. The monkey who desires the food, will put its hand inside the pot and take a big handful of the food. Thus the monkey becomes unable to draw its hand out through the opening. Only on releasing the grip will the monkey be able to take its hand out. It is its desire for the food that has bound its hands. Because it took with its hand some food to fulfil its desire, it was bound there. This wide world is like that pot and our 'samsaras' or families are like the narrow top. Our desires are the sweets in the pot. The world being pot, containing the desires, sweets, man puts his hand in the pot. When he sheds his desires, he will be able to live in the world freely. To get freedom, the first thing to do is to sacrifice. In philosophical terms, this is called renunciation. We think that the world is binding us but the world is lifeless. It is the desire that binds us.

YOUR THOUGHTS AFFECT THE FOOD YOU COOK

To purify the mind and the intellect for the correct reflection of the truth, the first caution is in regard to food. Indeed, this is a very serious matter for Sadhakas. There lived in Malur, Mysore, State, a pious Brahmin who was a great scholar. He had an equally pious wife. He was always intent on puja and japa-dhyana and was known far and wide for his virtuous character. One day, a sanyasin called Nityananda came to his door seeking alms; so, he was happy beyond measure. He invited the monk to take dinner with him the next day so that he might honour him with due hospitality. He hung green festoons over his doors and made elaborate arrangements for the reception. But, at the eleventh hour, physical impurity rendered his wife unfit to prepare food for the honoured guest or for any one else. A neighbour volunteered to cook the meal and she was brought in and introduced into the kitchen. Everything went off well and all were as happy as they could be, under the circumstances. Only, the sanyasin was wrung during meals by an overpowering desire to steal the silver cup which the host had placed near his plate. In spite of his best efforts, the evil idea won and the sanyasin hurried to his abode with the cup hidden in the folds of his robe. He could not sleep that night, for his conscience pricked him so. He felt he had brought disgrace on his Guru and on the rishis whom he invoked by the mantras he recited. He could not rest until he ran back into the Brahmin's house and, falling at his feet, restored the article with repentance trickling down his cheeks. Every one wondered how such a saint could stoop so low; then someone suggested it might be the fault transmitted to the food he ate, by the person who cooked it.. And when they examined the history of the neighbour they found that she was an irrepressible thief! The thieving tendency had, by subtle contact, affected the food she prepared. This is the reason why Sadhakas are advised to live on fruits and tubers only, when they reach a certain stage of spiritual achievement.

YAGNAS AND YAGAS ARE HIGHLY VALUABLE

Good deeds done in a dedicatory spirit do not add to the length or strength of Yama's rope; they give santi and santosha, in plenty. Why, you had a very good illustration of this just today. The final offering of sacred objects in the sacrificial fire of the Rudrayaga was done here at 10 A.M and, there was a welcome downpour of unexpected rain at 10.05 AM! Those who do not know the true values of yagna and yaga ridicule these rites and shout that they involve the loss of precious ghee and fuel, which could be put to better use. They do not realise that the food they themselves consume is a colossal waste, for, they do no good to the world or for themselves. The cigarettes are a waste, indeed, a dangerous waste; The bush coasts, the films they see, the radio

-hours they listen to are, all waste. You see a sculptor working away at a rock with his chisel and you condemn his work of chipping pieces as waste of precious time, and valuable stone. You do not know that one day a form of divine beauty will emerge. You see the ryot scatter valuable seeds on the mushy field; you blame him for wasting eatable stuff! You do not realise that he will harvest it a hundredfold in a few months. Your criticism is born of ignorance The rain that fell this morning and surprised every one did not surprise Me, for it is the inevitable consequence of the yaga. It is a special science, which pundits know; honour them for it.

STEADFASTNESS AND DEEP FAITH WIN THE GRACE OF GOD

When you have filled your heart with sympathy for the distressed, the lord will shower His grace. Draupadi had earned the grace through her devotion and virtues. Sita, too, stuck to the highest ideal of life, inspite of the severe suffering she underwent. Hanuman, who discovered her in the grove where she was kept as a prisoner by her abductor, offered to re cross the ocean with her on his shoulders and take her safe to her Lord, Rama. But she replied that she will not allow herself to be abducted back from the custody of Ravana, since that will deprive Rama of the chance to punish him for his crime and retriever her through his own heroism! Splendid words, these! Quite in consonance with the dictates of Dharma! No wonder, the Lord's Grace saved her in good time! If you have no steadfastness and no depth of faith, you can have no Grace.

UNCONCERN LEADS TO THE DEEPEST YEARNING FOR GOD

Sri Ramakrishna said that if you want to avoid the sticky fluid in the jack-fruit from contacting your fingers when you peel it, you have to apply a few drops of oil on them. So too, said he, " if you do not want the world and its reactions to stick to you, have a few drops of 'unconcern' applied on your mind".

The unconcern leads to the deepest yearning for God. Chaitanya went to Brindavan, where every particle of dust was sacred for him, since Krishna trod that soil centuries ago. He did not see or hear or touch or smell or taste anything expect Krishna at Brindavan. He was rendered so oblivious to the world around him that he ignored demands of hunger, thirst and social etiquette. He yearned for the consecrated food that was offered to Krishna in the temple . But, one night, the Lord appeared before him and admonished him for entertaining that one desire too! When at last, he gave up that desire also and was overwhelmed with the thirst for Him and Him alone, Krishna manifested before him, from within him. The Divine Chaitanya (consciousness) illuminated the Chaitanya in human form.

Learn therefore the discipline, that can make the mind settle on God only and never waver there from.

SUPERSTITIONS AND BLIND IMITATION

In the years gone by, every village home was stocked full of paddy bags, and so, rats too inevitably infested every home. In one such home, they were celebrating every full-moon day, the rite called Satyanarayana Puja. This required the collection of a good quantity of milk and ghee, the previous night itself. The rats attracted cats and the cats often preferred milk and ghee to the rodent food they are accustomed to. So, the milk and ghee were carefully kept in places, out of reach of the cats. But during the celebrations on the sacred day the milk and ghee had to be kept open and available for use, in vessels around the shrine. That was the chance for the depredatory cat; so the master of the house caught the cat by the neck and put it under a heavy basket, and placed a stone on it, so that it could not play any mischief with the holy offerings. This was done so consistently every full moon day as a safety measure in one home that the children and grandchildren felt that, puja or no puja, no full moon day should pass without a cat being imprisoned under a weighed basket! They started searching for a cat and bring it home, so that the ritual of the cat and basket could be observed without fail.

The original meaning and purpose was lost during the passage of time and later generations were burdened with a belief that danger lurks if a cat is not dealt with in the way of their fore-fathers! From being an insufferable nuisance, the cat rose to a new status of importance! This is blind imitation

IT IS NEVER TOO SOON IN THE SPIRITUAL REALM

There was once a miser who lived in a leaky house; the rain-water poured into the house through the roof but he sat through it all. Neighbours laughed at him and warned him to get the roof repaired. But in the rainy season he replied, "Let the rains subside, how can I repair it now?" And when the rains stopped, he replied, "Why should I worry about leaks, now the rains have stopped?" Do not suffer the leaks when the rains come, as they are sure to do; repair the roof now itself. That is to say, acquaint yourselves with the spiritual primers and textbooks now itself; begin the first lesson of silence, prayer, and chanting the Name of the Lord. It is never too soon in the spiritual realm.

TRANSISTOR RADIO-A BARBER'S BOX

It is the distorted sense of values that makes you carry a radio receiver strapped to your shoulder, even when you come to Prasanthi Nilayam! This has become a fashion; sons-in-law now try to extract a transistor radio from their fathers-in-law, as quickly as possible. There was a young man in a big town; it so happened that his father arrived on a visit and was received at the railway station by the son himself. They were going home in an auto-rickshaw, when the father, already confused by the roar and noise of the traffic, noticed some one carrying a small rectangular box, strapped to his shoulder. He saw many more such boxes, carried proudly by young men, fashionably attired and walking in strut, with a nonchalant gaze. He asked his son what they charged in the town for a shave and when the son answered, a half-rupee, he was surprised that it was so cheap. "These barbers going about with these boxes strapped on the shoulders are so well-dressed and rich looking that I thought they must be charging five rupees at least", he said. The poor man thought the transistor radio sets were barber's boxes! In fact, many who carry them and tune in do not know the A B C of music, eastern or western, nor do they know an iota of geography or history or politics to appreciate the news. They carry watches on their wrists but, to know what hour it is, they have to stretch their wrists before those sitting next to them! They cannot read a watch, nor have they any engagement to keep. All this is a needless multiplication of misery!

KABIR'S PITAMBARA FOR THE LORD

Kabir was weaving a pitambara for the Lord, his Rama. He had to work the loom alone by hand. He recited Rama Rama Rama Rama and went on weaving ceaselessly. The cloth had become twenty yards long, but, Kabir did not stop; his tapas continued unabated; the pitambara was becoming longer and longer. The Ananda of the craft, devotion to his Lord, were enough food and drink for his subsistence. When he gave it to the temple priest for clothing the idol of Rama, the pitambara was just the size, just the length and breadth, not a finger more !

"DHARMA BODHA"-TRUE DHARMA OF A MAHATMA

Samartha Ramadas appeared before Sivaji, with his usual call for alms: Bhavati Bhikshaam Dehi. Sivaji realised that the guru is God; so he wrote something on a piece of paper and deposited it reverentially in the alms-bag of Ramadas. For the relief of hunger, how can paper suffice? Asked Ramadas. Sivaji prayed that the paper may be read. The paper recorded a gift of the entire kingdom and all that Sivaji owned to the Guru. Samartha Ramadas replied: "No, my dharma is dharma-bodha, the teaching of dharma, instructing the people in the right way of life; Kshatriyas like you must follow the dharma of ruling the land, ensuring peace and content to the millions under your care". Yajnavalkya too once refused a kingdom, because he cared more for the kingdom of moksha, the realm of freedom. Vasishta is also said to have renounced a kingdom offered to him by Rama.

EVERY MATERIAL OBJECT HAS A QUALITATIVE AND QUANTITATIVE DIFFERENCE

By reading many books and developing an argumentative tendency, it is quite common today that young people get into argument with others. Once a young man aged 22 years went to Sankara. When Sankara was giving spiritual lessons to his disciples he interrupted and asked Sankara if all human beings in this wide world should not be regarded as equal since the same kind of blood flows in all of them. Sankara smiled at this young man and said that the blood flowing in that youngster is hot and fast and so he was trying to push things too far. It is not possible for man to distinguish between permanent and impermanent things. One can adopt the notion of non-duality or advaita in one's own thoughts and attitudes but it is not possible to equate everything in the world in practice. The young man insisted that this does not seem right. He stated that to him, the proper thing appeared to be to treat all living being in the same manner. Sankara recognised that if this young man was allowed to go on in this strain, he was likely to reach some absurd conclusions. Sankara decided at once to teach him a lesson and immediately asked whether he had a mother. The young man replied that he had a mother who was alive and that he respected her very much. He again asked if the young man was married. The young man replied that he was married and that his wife also had come with him to the ashram. Sankara then asked him if he had a mother-in-law. The young man replied that the mother-in-law was quite hale and healthy. Sankara again asked if he had any sisters and the young man replied in the affirmative and said he had two sisters. Sankara asked if all these people were women. The young man asked how it should be otherwise. Sankara asked if he regarded all of them as equal and was treating all these people in the same manner and if in particular, he was treating his wife as mother and his sister as his mother.

In this world of multiplicity one has to recognise qualitative and quantitative differences. Each electric bulb is varying in power and wattage. Therefore the light radiating from the bulb is not due to electric current. The current is the same everywhere but the difference arises from the bulbs with different intensities. God's power is like electric power and our bodies are the bulbs.

RABBIA MALIK AND HUSSAIN

Remember, your real nature is the same as the other man's; he is yourself known by another name. When you do a good deed, you are doing it to yourself; when you do a bad turn to some one, remember, you are injuring yourself; so, avoid doing evil to others. I am reminded what Hussain, the son of Rabbia Malik of Persia used to do. He rose early and went to the mosque for prayer with great diligence and devotion. When he came, he found the servants of the house still sleeping on their mats and he grew wild at them; he swore and cursed them for neglect of religious duties. Then his father chastised him. He said; "son, why do you get angry with those poor souls who are too tired to wake up early? Do not wipe off the good results of your adherence to the rule of God by falling foul of these innocent slaves. I wish you would much rather rise late and abstain from the mosque, for now you have grown proud that you are more religious than these others and you dare blame them for faults for which they are not themselves responsible".

FAITH AND SCIENCE

A Hindu and his British friend once happened to come to the Godavari. The Hindu said. "I will bathe in this sacred water". He recited the name "Hari" as he plunged in and came out refreshed in mind as well as body. He felt great happiness that he got the rare chance of a bath in the holy river. The Britisher laughed and said , "This is mere H_2O; how can you get unspeakable joy by dipping into it? It is all superstition". But the Hindu replied, "leave me to my superstition; you can stick to your superstition". The cynic got only physical cleanliness but the believer got mental purity also.

MAYA CAN RUIN A LIFE

Maya has the capacity to ruin our life. If we understand the nature of Maya well, it will go away from us in one moment. If we give high place to it without understanding, then that will get the upper hand and will begin to dance on our heads.

In one village a marriage was to take place. The party of the bridegroom came to the village and was staying in a house. The party of the bride was staying in another house. In between these two parties, there was one individual who wanted all kinds of comforts and was demanding them from both the parties. This individual used to go to the bridegroom's place and tell them that they were always coming and causing a lot of problems to the bride's party. People belonging to the bridegroom's party thought that he was some respected elder from the side of the bride. Similarly he went to the bride's house and told them that they were not respecting the bridegroom and members of his party and were not giving them all the respect that was due to them. This individual was enacting a drama. He was going to the bridegroom's party and was behaving as if he was a respected elder from the bride's side and was going to the bride's people and behaving as if he was a respected elder from the bridegroom side. When this drama went too far, the two parties started investigating and found that he belonged to neither side. Once you make an enquiry and find out the origin of Maya, it will disappear, even as the individual in our story disappeared .

AFFECTION AND ATTACHMENT RESPONSIBLE FOR JOYS AND SORROWS

Moha expresses itself in desiring things. Desires go on multiplying. Moha may be compared to the water that is found in a lake.

I will now give an example. There is a girl in one house. There is young man in another house, their houses are almost side by side . But girl does not know anything about the young man, and the young man does not know anything about the girl living in the neighbouring house. One day, the girl fell seriously ill . That day all the people in the house were hectic and they were all anxious and several doctors were called in. When the boy in the neighbouring house heard the noise, he thought it was a disturbance to his studies, and, therefore, he closed his window and started reading. But in course of time, as a result of destiny, this boy who was living in that house got married to that girl in the neighbouring house. The marriage took place in the morning. In the afternoon the girl developed a stomach ache and this bridegroom felt very anxious for the girl and her stomach ache. Where and when had he developed this attachment to the girl? Because he got married to her, even a little stomach ache upsets him now. Though the same girl fell dangerously ill some time ago, he did not feel even the slightest anxiety for her because at that time there was no attachment or relationship with that girl. So, abhimana and mamakara, affection and attachment, are responsible for all joys and sorrows.

SECRET OF A HAPPY FAMILY

At one time there was a severe famine in Bihar. A family consisting of father, mother and two children started from Bihar to find livelihood elsewhere. The father of the family being responsible to feed this family underwent many difficulties and hardships. He even starved himself on some occasions and because of this frequent starvation, he died after sometime. The mother having lost her husband, suffered from loneliness and had to bear the burden of keeping the family alive in this wide world. She went begging from house to house and if she got some and if it was not enough, she starved and let her children eat. In course of time, she became so debilitated that she found it difficult to walk from house to house and beg. The little boy of twelve looked at the pitiable sight of his mother and sitting on her lap said, "Oh mother, please take rest for some time. I shall beg and bring food for you". As she listened to the words of her son, her heart melted. She felt very miserable that she had to send her son to beg for food. No mother wants her child to become a beggar. Because the boy insisted, the mother consented. From that day the boy was begging for food and giving it to his mother and the little brother and he himself would starve. After some days, he felt he could not walk and go out for begging. He went to a house and found the master of the house reading a news paper sitting on an easy chair. In a feeble voice, he asked the master for food. The master replied that it would be useless to give alms and said that he would give him food on a leaf. The boy, out of weakness, fainted. The master of the house lifted the boy and put him on his lap. The boy sat mumbling some words. To be able to understand what he was saying, the master put his ear close to the mouth of the boy. The boy was inaudibly whispering, "The food that you wish to give, please give it first to my mother". After uttering those last words, he passed away.

We do not now find this kind of love , this intimate love existing between the members of a family. Here we find that the head of the family starved himself to death for the sake of the family; The mother starved herself for the sake of her children and son starved and killed himself to save his mother from begging. Look at this example of affection that bound together as father, mother and child they look like the Holy Trinity. Therefore, each member of the family must discharge his own responsibility.

RICHES ARE A DEADLY TEMPTATION

The desire to raise the standard of life is a thirst that can never be quenched. It leads to endless pursuit of sensory pleasure, multiplication of wants, deeper and deeper involvement in worry. Riches are a deadly temptation. No Whip can suppress the itch to gain money. Once, Lakshmi (the goddess of wealth) and Narayana (her lord) had a quarrel over who was supreme in the heart of mankind. They decided to settle it by means of an experiment. Lakshmi came down among mankind as a spiritual teacher; when people washed her feet and worshipped her, the plate and vessels used by the devotees turned into gold ! So, she was welcomed everywhere and there was a terrible rush of devotees and a huge pile of brass, copper and aluminium vessels in evidence everywhere ! Meanwhile, Narayana too was upon the earth as an exponent of the sacred scriptures expounding to the huge gatherings the paths to happiness and joy, marked out by the sages. When the people heard of Lakshmi converting metal into gold, they preferred her visits to those of Narayana and cared little for what he thought. He was actually sent out of cities and villages when Lakshmi entered them, for his discourses distracted them from the profitable sessions of Lakshmi Puja.

ENSLAVE YOURSELF TO GOD AND NOT MAN

Maintain your self-respect as Draupadi did. When she was about to be humiliated in the open court, where her husbands, who had staked her and lost her in dice-play to the wicked Kauravas, were present. She was so enraged that if she had only cast a look on the gang of the ruffians who had won her and dragged her thither, they would have collapsed into heaps of ash; instead, she looked at Dharmaraja, the eldest husband who had staked her and who was sitting before her with downcast eyes. That looked quietened her a little. Then she uttered a curse, which echoed over earth and heaven. " May the wives of these vipers who laid their hand on my hair and dragged me here, lament their widowhood, waving their loosened hair, in inconsolable grief. Until then, I shall not plait the hair which these barbarians have unloosened now". She proclaimed, in the hearing of all, her lineage, and its reputation for self-respect and her resolve not to tarnish it or demean it. Maintain the dignity of your lineage of Rama, Krishna, Harishchandra, Mira, Tyagaraja, Tukaram. Ramakrishna, Nandanar. The glory of your lineage is like a carefully rolled ball of thread. Any slip on your part will result in its disastrous entanglement. So beware ! Enslave yourself to God and not man. Hold fast to your sadhana.

RASAKRIDA - ITS SIGNIFICANCE

When you dedicate yourselves to the glorification of the Lord, you will revere the body, the senses, the intelligence, the will, and all the instruments of knowledge, action and feelings as essential for His work. While others will get intoxicated with pride, the bhaktha or devotee will be intoxicated with prema, unadulterated love. You have heard that when the Divine Cowherd Boy played on the flute, the men, women and children and even the cattle of Brindavan hurried to him, as if drawn by the irresistible magic of His music, Divine Melody, that stills all the turbid waves which we name as joy and grief. They left the work they were engaged in; they had no other thought than the attainment of the Divine presence; the cattle stopped grazing; the calves stopped guzzling milk. The story of Krishna and the Gopis or cowherds has a deep inner meaning. Brindavan is not a definite place on map, it is the universe itself. All men are cowherds; all animals are cows. Every heart is filled with the longing for the Lord; the flute is the call of the Lord; the sport called Rasakrida (the sportive dance; the dance of Krishna in His boyhood with the cowherdesses), in which Lord Krishna is described as dancing with the milkmaids in the moonlight- every maid has a boy-Krishna holding her hand in the dance- is the symbol of the yearning and the travail, borne by those who aim at reaching His presence. The Lord manifests such grace, that each one of you has the Lord all for yourself; you need not be sad that you won't have Him, when the others get Him; nor need you be proud that you have Him and no one else can have Him at the same time ! The Lord is installed in the altar of your heart.

STICK TO YOUR INNATE NATURE - WHATEVER MAY HAPPEN

A hermit was one day bathing in the Ganga, when he saw a scorpion. This is God encased in the scorpion form and name, he felt; he wanted to save the scorpion. So, he took it on his palm, but, when it stung him, he dropped it on the waters. Then he was stricken with remorse and so, he lifted it up again. Thus it stung him five or six times; but, he persisted in his mission of mercy and at last, managed to drop it on dry land so that it could go its way, alive and happy. Many people who watched his efforts laughed at him for his stupidly exaggerated sympathy. The hermit told them that the scorpion had taught him a lesson and he was thankful for it. They asked, what? He said, "stick to your innate nature, whatever may happen- that is what it has taught me". Its nature is to sting, regardless of whom or when. Man's nature is to achieve Jnana; Ananda is man's essence; Love is the blood - stream that sustains him; peace is the vision that guides and directs him. That is the reason why he is addressed as ' Amritasya Putra', in the Upanishads: he is the son of immorality; he has no birth, no death.

PERFORM ALL WORK INTELLIGENTLY

There was a pundit who taught grammar and rhetoric to a group of pupils. After finishing a course of lessons, he gave them an assignment; to compose four lines of poetry. One young man, who struggled with himself to produce an appropriate rhyme, had the first two lines.

The Full Moon is shining bright.
The tree has fruits at height,

and in his despair, he completed the quartrain with two more lines, more absurd than those two;

The food is not cooked aright !
Ganganna's face is a horried sight !

The assignment of course is completed; but how futile, how pathetic, how worthless the result! Most of you fulfil live's assignment as absurdly as this!

ACT RIGHT, THEN CLAIM THE FRUIT

There is a story of some monkeys which planted a mango garden. They planted the saplings, watered them a few days, and plucked them from off the ground to see how deep the roots had gone ! They wanted them to grow fast and yield fruits, but they were unaware of the process by which alone they could get the fruits they craved for ! Act right; then, claim the fruit. Cultivate with care; and collect the harvest.

WORDS REVEAL THE BREEDING OF THE SPEAKER

The tongue is the index of true breeding. " Hey ! You clout! Did you hear soldiers march this way? " A man asked a blind farmer. Minutes later another person accosted him, " Blind man ! Open your mouth and tell me whether you heard the noise of soldiers marching this way". Later, a third voice approached him, " Sir, did you hear some soldiers marching along this path ?" At last, another person came near and placed his hand upon his shoulder, " My dear man, please tell me whether you heard men marching along this road? " The blind man correctly described his interrogators as a soldier, a captain, a minister and the king himself. The words reveal the breeding of the speaker. The tongue is the armour of the heart; it guards one's life. Loud talk, long talk, wild talk, full of anger and hate, all these affect the health of man. They breed anger and hate in others; they wound, they excite, they enrage, they estrange. Why is silence said to be golden? The silent man has no enemies, though he may not have friends. He has the leisure and the chance to dive within himself and examine his own faults and failings. He has no more any inclination to seek them in others. If your foot slips, you earn a fracture; if your tongue slips you fracture some one's faith or joy. That fracture can never be set right; that wound will fester for ever. Therefore use the tongue with great care. The softer you talk, the less you talk, the sweeter you talk, the better for you and the world.

ABSORB ONLY GOOD IDEAS FROM SATSANG

Many people do not imbibe good ideas from good com pany because they hold on to their prejudices, preconceived ideas and preoccupations. To them, Kumbhakarna sends message of sleep and they go to sleep, while others who are awake are troubled by extraneous thoughts of their office and so on . Yet others keep on looking hither and thither, and therefore only a small minority of participants absorbe the good ideas from satsang.

At one time, there was a pandit who was expounding the Ramayana and he undertook to do this for a period of seven days. A woman, who had recently lost her husband, used to attend the same for some solace. She was a regular visitor and used always to sit in the front row. The Pundit was expounding the Ramayana every day and this woman was constantly looking at the book and shedding tears. The Pundit presumed that she had great devotion and so at the end of the seven days, he announced that because of her regular attendance and devotion, he would give the prasad first to her. While doing so, he asked her if she had enjoyed the discourses on Ramayana. In great sorrow, the lady replied that she did not know whether the Pundit was reciting Mahabharatha or Ramayana. She further said that she was however in great grief, because the black string at the back of the book was reminding her of the string which her late husband used to wear around his waist. Thus she conveyed that her tears had nothing to do with the Pundit's exposition of Ramayana !

HAPPINESS AND YOUR THINKING

It all depends on the point of view whether you are happy or unhappy, that colours all attitudes and opinions. Ramadas sang about the exploits of Anjaneya in Lanka and , while doing so, he mentioned the white lilies of the islands. Anjaneya heard him sing it and immediately took exception to the description. He said that he had never seen a single white flower there; the lilies of Lanka were red, he declared. Ramadas, however insisted that they were white. Anjaneya got annoyed at the impudence of poets who tried to pit their imagination against a firsthand expert witness and appealed to Rama for intercession. Rama agreed with Ramadas ! He said that Anjaneya saw them red because, his eyes were affected by Rajasic anger at the entire Rakshasa brood!

IMPLICIT FAITH IS THE ROAD TO SPIRITUAL SUCCESS

Once Krishna and Arjuna were going together along the open road. Seeing a bird in the sky, Krishna asked Arjuna: " Is that a dove ? " He replied, " Yes, it is a dove. " He told Arjuna. "It is an eagle". Arjuna replied promptly, " Yes, it is an eagle. " "No, Arjuna, it looks like a crow to Me. Is it not a crow? " asked Krishna. Arjuna replied, " I am sorry, it is a crow beyond doubt" . Krishna laughed and chided him for his agreeing to whatever suggestion was given. But Arjuna, said, " For me, Your Words are far more weighty than the evidence of my eyes: you can make it a crow, dove or an eagle and when you say it is a crow, it must be one." Implicit faith is the road to spiritual success.

MOTHER KALI BLESSES TENALI RAMAKRISHNA

Tenali RamaKrishna, the famous Andhra poet, humorist and philosopher, once happened to lose his way while traversing an area of thick jungle. You know that he lived in the reign of the famous Emperor Krishnadeva Raya, of the Vijayanagara Dynasty, about 1500 A.D. He was attached to the Court and was honoured as a wise and quick-witted minister. While he was wandering desperately in the jungle, he saw an old sage. Ramakrishna ran forward and fell at his feet, in reverential homage. He asked the sage, how he got caught in that wild forest. The sage said , " the same mysterious force that dragged you here has dragged me too to this spot. The moment when I have to cast away the body I occupied so long, has arrived ! I shall initiate you, now, into the mantra which I have recited all these years, as my talisman and treasure" . It was the mantra of Mother Kali, and he whispered it into the ear of Ramakrishna.

Ramakrishna was overjoyed at the great gift; he retired into a temple of the mother, deep in the recesses of the jungle and was intent on the meditation of the Mother, propitiated by the Mantra. At midnight one day, aboriginal Koyas of the forest came into the temple, with a goat which they sought to offer as sacrifice to please Her and propitiate Her. Ramakrishna hid behind the idol and when the knife was about to fall on the neck of the victim, he exclaimed, " I am the Mother of all the living beings including you. If you kill my child, I will curse you, I cannot bless you !" believing that it was Kali that spoke, the Koyas desisted and went away.

Now, Kali manifested before Ramakrishna. She asked him, what he liked to receive from Her ! She was pleased with his sadhana. "Which do you want ? " She queried, holding a plate of curd-rice in one hand and a plate of milk-rice in another. He wanted to know the consequences of eating either plate before deciding which plate to ask for. She explained. " The curd-rice will endow you with riches and economic prosperity; the milk-rice will make you a wise scholar. Now, make your choice". Ramakrishna thought within himself. "It is not good being a fool in possession of vast riches; nor, will scholarship fill the stomach, three times a day" . He was a clever person ! So, he asked a further question: " I see two plates before me . Before I make the choice, tell me how each will taste".

She laughed and said," how can I describe the taste and make you understand the difference ? You will have to taste them your self" and gave him both the plates, for the purpose.

The clever Ramakrishna hastily put them both in his mouth and managed to swallow the curds and the milk, the entire quantity of rice from both plates !

Kali was indignant and exclaimed that his impertinence called for dire punishment. Ramakrishna accepted his mistake and invited the punishment she proposed to inflict. But , can the Mother's punishment destroy the child, however reprehensible the conduct of the child may be?

"My sentence will certainly save you, do not tremble", said Kali. Then she pronounced the sentence thus: " Become a Vikatakavi". That is to say," Be a clever clown, having great influence at court accumulating much wealth and guiding all those who approach you with good advice."

God loves those who have self-confidence and courage of conviction and who seize every opportunity to improve their spiritual status.

THIS WORLD IS A PART OF KALPAVRIKSHA

Because God comes out of our heart in the form of speech, we must try to make our speech as pure and as clean as possible. God is also in the form of truth. So, whatever we will be saying will have an echo: "Let it be so !" There is a small story for this. A traveller was going on his way. After going some distance he was tired on account of the summer heat. By the side of the path there was a big tree and he went there to take rest under the shade of the tree. When he went into that cool shade , he was over joyed. Then he said to himself, " I am able to find a very cool place; how fortunate will I be if I will be able to get a glass of cool water also here ? " Instantaneously, a tumbler of water came down. After he drank that water, he thought, "Now I have quenched my thirst, how happy will I be if there is a good bed here because this floor is hard and rough". At once a big soft bed came down. He then thought," Even in my house, I do not possess such a pillow. If my wife comes here and sees, how happy will she feel? " Immediately the wife also came. He saw her and he thought " Is she my wife or is she a demon ? Will she eat me? " No sooner he said this, she ate him. The tree under the shade of which he sat is ' Kalpavriksha'. Kalpavriksha is a tree that fulfils all desires. When the traveller sat under the Kalpavriksha, what ever good things he thought of, he got them instantly. But when he thought about bad things, bad things also came to him. This world is a part of Kalpavriksha. We are sitting under the shade of this Kalpavriksha. If we think badly, bad happens to us and if we think in a good manner good happens to us. So when our thoughts, when our contemplation and when our deeds are pure, the Kalpavriksha of the world will be giving the good things desired by us. Both good and bad will come only from our heart. They never come from out side. That is why in the beginning we have to make our heart as pure as possible.

GURU HAS TO BE HIMSELF BRAHMAN

There was a seeker once who prayed to his elder brother to initiate him into spiritual life, with the imparting of a saving mantra; but, the brother said, "It is always a hard job to teach one's kinsman, and to teach a brother is harder still. You should go to Dakshinamurthy, who is Siva himself come as teacher." The brother inquired how to discover that preceptor. Then the brother said, " He who considers all men and all things equal- he is the preceptor I have indicated". So the young man started his search. He went among the hermitages with a gold ring on his finger; he interrogated the hermits, what the metal was. Some declared it was gold, some brass, some copper, others said it was tin or some alloy. So, he moved on. Then, he came upon a young ascetic with shining eyes. He asked him whether it was gold. The ascetic said , 'Yes.' He said , ' Is it not brass? ' He replied, 'Yes it is brass'

He said 'yes', to whatever he said it was. He could not recognise any distinction. So, the young man concluded that the ascetic before him was Dakshinamurthy. Equanimity comes as a result of the awareness of the unity, not otherwise. Sanat Kumar was engaged in extreme austerity when God appeared before him. He asked to place before him his needs. But Sanat Kumar said, " You are my guest now. You have come to this place, where I am since some time; so you may ask anything you need; I am bound to honour the guest, granting him what he needs" . Having known Brahman he had become Brahman Himself. So he could talk as an equal to God. ' I am you' , that was the stage reached by Sanat Kumar. No wonder he spoke like that. He is ever present; I is born only after the individual separates himself from the He. So, with the birth of the Jiva, the idea of Deva or God must also be born in the mind. That is the sign of safety and success.

THE DIKSHA FOR ACQUIRING RAKSHA

The Lord is all compassion, all grace. Bhishma the grandfather of both the clans that were battling for supremacy in the field of Kurukshetra, had led the Kaurava hosts for eight days, but victory was not in sight. So the eldest of the Kauravas, Duryodhana approached him and prayed for a more terrific onslaught on the enemy to be guided and directed by him. Bhishma replied that it would be either death or victory for him, the next day. Knowing this, Krishna persuaded the Pandava queen Draupadi, who was imbued with the deepest devotion to him, to accompany Him to the camp of Bhishma at dead of night. Prayer was the source of strength for that tormented queen; her prayers could not but move the lord. She entered the tent of Bhishma with her face hidden behind a veil. Krishna had asked her to leave her sandals behind, lest their pit-a-pat should disturb the silence and alert the guardsmen. He wrapped them in a silken kerchief and carried the bundle under His arm !

Draupadi moved into the tent and fell at the feet of Bhishma, who blessed her, automatically, as was his wont, "May you have many years of happy married life!" Drapupadi revealed herself as soon as she was blessed thus; she prayed that the Pandava brothers, her husbands, may be saved from his arrows. Bhishma guessed that Krishna must be the originator of this stratagem; Bhishma knew that he was doomed to die. "We are but puppets in His hands" he said and when he found Him at the entrance to the tent, he inquired what the bundle contained. Imagine his feelings when he was told that the lord had condescended to carry under His arms, the sandals worn by His devotee ! Have faith in Him; He will never give you up; He will guard and guide, until victory is won. Sincere devotion, unshaken faith they can never fail to earn grace.

Draupadi had the faith to surrender unreservedly; she led a dedicated life. The five Pandava brothers who were her husbands are the vital airs, the Pancha-prana which activate and vitalise the body. She is energy that sustains the pranas, by constant vigilant care.

To have that faith you must dive deep into the inner mystery of the avataras like Rama or Krishna, and not lose your way in the tangle of the outer events and emotional conflicts, the external adventures and activities. Do not take Rama as a brother, son, husband, entangled in the personal calamity of having his wife kidnapped and heroically rescuing her. You can be moved into adoration only by diving into the cool depths of the inner mystery. This process was specially discovered by the sages of India, and so India rose to the status of the guru of the whole world. Incessant humility, insistent reverence, contemplation on God and His glory-these shall be your Diksha (path of dedication) for acquiring Raksha (security).

THE LORD WILL NOT BE SILENT WHEN THE BHAKTHA IS INSULTED

There was in Bengal a bhaktha named Madhavadasa, who realised when his wife died that he had lost his 'home', for his grihalakshmi had passed away; so he gave all his riches to the poor, donned a gerua robe and wandered alone as a pilgrim to the Jagannatha shrine. There he did such deep penance that the concrete image soon became the Abstract reality and the Abstract reality became a perpetual vision. He lost all sense of time and space, of chith and achith. Then the Lord, with Subhadra, His Sakthi Aspect, moved towards him and placed before him the gold plate used by the priests to keep food in front of Jagannatha in the sanctum sanctorum. When Madhavadasa awoke to his gross surroundings, he saw the gold plate with the pile of delicious food upon it; he ate his fill and returned to his inner paradise which he had left for a while.

Meanwhile, the plate was reported lost, assumed to be stolen, and discovered by the seashore near madhavadasa, who was promptly arrested and led to the lockup by some very efficient policemen. He was beaten mercilessly but did not seem to mind it a bit. The chief priest that night had a dream in which Jagannatha asked him not to bring food for the Lord again into the shrine, for: "You bring food for me, and when I eat it, you start beating me !" Then he realised that it was all the Lord's leela to demonstrate the devotion of Madhavadasa and teach others the real nature of bhakthi.

Some scholars and pundits of Puri did not feel happy at this sudden rise to fame of a stranger from Bengal: so they called Madhavadasa into their midst and challenged him to an intellectual duel. Madhavadasa was not a pundit of that type: he had learnt the sastras only as a staff to help him walk, as a guide to action: not as a stick to beat others with. So he accepted defeat even before the bout began and signed a statement to that effect, which the leading pundit was only too glad to accept because Madhavadasa had a reputation for scholarship which was really frightening. The pundit hurried to Kasi with that token of victory: he waved it before a gathering of scholars and demanded that they should all pay him homage as superior even to Madhavadasa. But the Lord will not allow His bhaktha to be humiliated. When the signed statement was opened and read, they were all amazed to find that it was a statement declaring that it was Madhavadasa who had achieved victory and it was the pundit who had signed underneath acknowledging his own defeat! The Lord will not be silent when the bhaktha is insulted or harmed.

THE LORD'S NAME AND THE CHAIN OF DESTINY CANNOT CO-EXIST

There was a great saint in Kerala some 500 years ago, Bilvamangala by name. He would call on Krishna and Krishna would appear. Such was his Bhakthi and his sadhana. One man who suffered from chronic stomach-ache heard about this and he pestered Bilvamangala to find out from Krishna whether it would end or not. Bilvamangala agreed and when Krishna appeared next, he asked Him the question. Krishna replied, "When the rolling stops, it will cease. The unfortunate man interpreted it to mean "when he stopped rolling in pain" and he got desperate, because he had perforce to roll in the agony of that ache. So he left Kerala and wanted to go to some holy place to meet some holier person who would procure for him a more satisfying answer. Bilvamangala told him that he had to suffer this trouble due to his prarabdha; that is, the result of his activities in previous births. He took rolling to mean, "rolling from birth to birth".

On the road to Kasi which he took, he came to a free feeding place run by a pious, lady, Kururamma by name. When she saw his agony, she spoke to him kindly. He told her that he had decided to drown himself in the Ganga for he was told there was no escaping the consequence of past sins. Kururamma called him a fool. She gave him the holy manthra, "Gopijanavallabhaya Namah", and asked him to repeat it. She said the name would cure him completely. The poor man uttered it when the attack occurred next and he was surprised to find that the pain had gone ! Yes, gone; even though he pounded his stomach, it did not return. He finished his pilgrimage to Kasi and returned to kerala and fell at the feet of Bilvamangala, who enquired about his ache with which he had to live, for it was earned in past lives. When he was told that it had disappeared, he called on Krishna and asked what he had meant by "rolling". Bilvamangala thought it to mean rolling from one birth to another and aquiring good and evil; the sick man took it to mean rolling in pain when the ache came on. But Krishna had meant rolling in this objective world, this Prakrithi and its changing Phenomena. When the man lived in the name of god and had no other thought, the rolling had ceased; the name and the chain of destiny cannot exist together. Prarabdha will melt away like fog before the sun when Namasmarana is done. This was a revelation even for Bilvamangala.

ISWARA SANKALPA WILL ALWAYS BE FULFILLED

I shall tell you the story of Iswara-sankalpa and how nothing could stop its realisation. Siva was every day discoursing on Kailasa to sages and saints and Devas in the evening hours. One day, Parvathi suggested that a hall be constructed for accommodating them all, so that they could all listen without being affected by the constant fog and mist and cold winds. Siva did not have the Sankalpa to put it up; still, Parvathi insisted that her idea must be implemented. The astrologer, who was consulted before the foundations were dug, said that "The stars forecast that the Hall will be consumed by fire, since Sani is not propitious from the very beginning". The hall was completed, nevertheless. Now, that set a problem for the couple. Siva proposed to ask Sani for the favour of saving the hall from his anger, though he doubted whether the planet, reputed for his inevitable ire, would ever agree. Parvathi felt deeply hurt and she resolved not to give the tiny tyrant, Sani, the credit for destroying the hall that she had got built. She swore that instead of giving him the chance to declare arrogantly that he had set fire to the hall, she would herself set fire to it. But Siva asked her to first await the outcome of his appeal to Sani; for He was Himself proceeding to His headquarters ! He told her, "If Sani agrees to exempt the hall from his anger, I shall come back and report the good news to you; but if he is adamant, I shall raise my hand and twirl this Dakka. On hearing that signal, you may set fire to the hall and rob Sani of the credit for doing so". Parvathi was ready with a burning torch in anticipation of the signal, so that there may not be a moment's chance for the wicked planet to execute his nefarious plan of revenge. Sani, however, agreed to the request made by Siva; he said that he would not burn down the hall in Kailasa and Siva was happy at his reply. So, when Sani prayed that he may be granted one small boon, Siva agreed and asked him what it was. It seems Sani had never before seen the famous dance of Siva which all the stellar divinities were extolling and Sani craved that Siva may show him a step or two. Siva readily assented and started the Thandava dance, raising His Hand and sounding Dakka ! Listening to the signal, Parvathi applied the torch and the hall was, as per the sankalpa of Siva, burnt to ashes ! Divine sankalpa must be fulfilled. Sani was just a tool in the divine plan.

YOGAKSHEMAM VAHAAMYAHAM

This statement about the Lord guaranteeing the Yogakshema of the devotee has given rise to a great deal of misunderstanding. Even pundits, not to speak of others, have failed to grasp its real import.

A learned pundit was once giving discourses on the Gita in the august presence of a Maharaja. One day, the turn of this sloka came :

Ananyaaschinthayantho maam
Ye janaah paryupaasathe
Theshaam nithyaabhiyukthaanaam
Yogakshemam vahaamyaham.

The pundit was explaining enthusiastically the manysided implications of this sloka, but the Maharaja shook his head and said: "This meaning is not correct". He continued to dispute the correctness of every one of the explanations the pundit gave. The poor pundit had won meritorious distinctions at the court of many a Maharaja and was honoured by them all with pompous titles. He felt as if he was stabbed when the Maharaja in the presence of the entire band of courtiers condemned his explanation of this sloka as 'wrong'. He smarted under the insult; but plucking up courage, he again set upon his task, and collecting all his scholarship, he plunged into an eloquent discourse on the multiple meaning of the words, "Yoga" and "kshema". The Maharaja did not approve of even this; he ordered; "find out the meaning of this sloka and having understood it well, come to me again tomorrow". With this, the Maharaja rose from his throne and went into the inner apartments.

The pundit lost even the few grains of courage left in him. He was weighed down by anxiety; he tottered under the insult, he reached home and, placing the copy of the Gita aside, he fell on the cot.

Surprised at this, the pundit's wife said, "Tell me why you came home from the palace today in such grief ? What exactly did happen ?" she rained one anxious question after another, so that the pundit was obliged to describe to her all that had happened, the insults heaped on his head, the command with which the Maharaja had sent him home etc. The wife listened calmly to the account of what had happened and after pondering deeply over the incident, she said, "yes; it is true. What the Maharaja said is right. The explanation you have for that sloka is not the correct one. How could the Maharaja approve it ? The fault is yours". At this, the pundit rose in anger from the cot, like a cobra whose tail is trodden hard. "What do you know, you silly woman ? Am I inferior in intelligence to you ? Do you, who are engaged in the kitchen all the time, cooking and serving, claim to know more than I ? Shut you mouth and quit my presence", he roared.

But the lady stood her ground; she replied, "Lord ! Why do you fly into such a rage at a statement of mere truth ? Repeat the sloka once again to yourself and ponder over its meaning. You will then arrive at the right answer yourself." Thus, by her soft words the wife brought calm into the mind of her husband.

The pundit started analysing the meaning of each individual word in the sloka. Ananyaaschinthayantho maam, he began, deliberately and slowly, repeating around the various meanings. The wife intervened and said, "What benefit is it to learn and expound the meanings of words ? Tell me what your intention was, when you approached this Maharaja. What was the purpose ?" At this pundit got wild. Sould I not run this family, this home ? How am I to meet the cost of food and drink, of clothes and things, for you and all the rest ? It is for the sake of these that I went to him, of course; or else, what business have I with him ?" he shouted.

The wife then replied. "If you had only understood what lord Krishna has declared in this sloka, the urge to go to this Maharja would not have arisen ! If He is worshipped without any other thought, if one but surrenders to Him, if at all times the mind is fixed on Him, then the lord has declared in this sloka that He would provide every thing for the devotee. You have not done these three; You approach the Maharaja, believing that he would provide everything ! That is where you have gone against the meaning of this verse. That is the reason why he did not accept your explanation".

Hearing this, that reputed scholar sat a while, ruminating on her remarks; he realised his fault; he did not proceed to the palace the next day. Instead he got immersed in the worship of Krishna at home. When the king inquired why the pundit had not appeared, courtiers said that he was staying at home and had not started out. The king sent a messenger, but the pundit declined to move out. He said, "There is no need for me to go to any one; my Krishna will provide me with everything; He will bear my yogakshema Himself. I suffered insult because I did not realise this so long, being blinded by eagerness to know the manifold meanings of mere words. Surrendering to Him, if I am ceaselessly engaged in worshipping Him, He will himself provide me with all I need".

When the messenger took this message to the palace, the Maharaja proceeded to the dwelling of the pundit, on foot; he fell at the feet of the pundit, saying "I thank you sincerely for explaining to me this day, out of your own experience, the meaning of the sloka which you expounded yesterday". Thus, the king taught the pundit that any propagation of spiritual matters which does not come out of the crucible of experience is mere glitter and show.

PRAYERS MUST EMANATE FROM THE HEART

Listen to what happened to sage Ramadas of Bhadrachalam, the singer who was imprisoned by the Nawab of Golconda, for misappropriation of public funds (to renovate the Rama temple at Bhadrachalam), whose liberation from jail was effected by Rama and Lakshmana themselves paying the Nawab the sum appropriated !

Ramadas had piled up a large mass of palmyra leaves, on each of which he had written with his stylo a song on Rama. When his eyes fell on the heap one day, a thought struck him; "Did I compose these songs for my pleasure ? Or, for pleasing Rama ?" He wanted to know those songs which had pleased Rama, and fling away those which did not. He decided to throw the whole bundle into the Godavari river, and let Rama save those which He approved. Almost the whole lot sank in the depths; only 108 floated and were rescued. They alone had arisen from the heart; the rest smacked of cleverness, artificiality, punditry, pedantry. Prayers must emanate from the heart, where god resides and not from the head, where doctrines and doubts clash.

WHO IS A REAL BHAKTHA ?

There is the story of a rustic who sat among a gathering of devotees and listened to the exposition of the Gita by a great pundit. All were wonder-struck by the scholarly commentary which the pundit gave and his learned disquisition on each word and phrase; and the rustic, though the exposition was very much over his head, seemed to attend very closely for he was all the time in tears ! When at last the pundit asked him why he was weeping, he surprised every body by the sincerity of his Bhakthi. For, he said that he wept at the predicament of the lord, who had to sit at the head of the chariot and half turning his neck hold forth so long to convince the dull-witted Arjuna. "How much pain must he be suffering in his neck?" He asked and wept. That was real devotion, a sure passport to spiritual victory. He had identified himself with participants in the episode and the whole setting had become alive for him.

ATMA DISCRIMINATES BEST

Buddhi or intelligence exhibits greater discrimination than the senses and atma exhibits greater discrimination than Buddhi. In one village there were two beggars. One was blind and the other lame. The two of them became friends. The blind had his feet and the lame had his eyes. They came to an agreement. The lame man climbed on the back of the blind man and gave directions like a steering wheel. On going from one village to another, they came to a field of cucumbers. The blind one asked if there was a fence or watchman around and the lame man said that there were none. The blind man then said that if the cucumbers were really good, no farmer would leave them like that in a field without a fence around or without a watchman. This meant that the cucumbers probably would be bitter to eat. The blind man could easily find out the truth of the matter because he had intelligence. This is the exercise of buddhi. The senses cannot determine the difference between good and bad. Buddhi can discriminate but not implement because it does not have the senses.

STUDINESS AND RITUALISM MUST GO WITH DISCRIMINATION IN SADHANA

There was a great Bhaktha once who failed in a test and so could not get the certificate. Every day at noon, he used to look out for a needy guest whom he could feed lavishly. Thus he spent years, but one day, a frail old figure toddled into the house and sat for the dinner. He had crossed the century mark in years. The host had the steadiness of the vow, but he did not have the discrimination to derive the fruit of that vow. Like water poured on a dry sand-bed, it did not add to its fertility. His heart still remained a dry sand-bed, though the waters of charity were poured on it every noon. The viveka-less heart drank up the charity and he was the same strict ritualist. The decrepit guest was overwhelmed by hunger and so, as soon as the first dish was served he swallowed a big morsel without reciting the name of god. Annoyed at this atheism, the host cursed the old man and pushed him out of doors to starve or beg in the hot sun. That night, he had a dream where the Lord chastised him for the cruelty of his behaviour. The Lord said, "For more than a hundred years, I nourished that man lovingly as the apple of my eye, though he never once took a single one of my many names. My dear man, could you not have suffered him for a few minutes ?".

PLAY HARISCHANDRA OR LANKADAHANA-NOT BOTH

I shall tell you what happened in a certain village. One section had specialised in acting the drama, Lanka-dahana; but the other section decided to enact the play Harischandra instead. For the role of Chandramathi, the queen, they had to select a person from the Lankadahana group, because they had no alternative actor at all. The scenes were following one after the other. All went well until the prince died of snake bite; then the mother refused to weep ! The "son" belonged to the opposite group. So vengeance was taken on Chandramathi by Harischandra. He rained blows on her for being so callous; the drama sped along in another course, the course of hatred and faction.

Thereupon, the Anjaneya of the Lankadahana group brought things to a climax by jumping on the stage in his role with a tail burning at one end; and he set the theatre on fire to the delight of his henchmen and the consternation of his rivals. You must play either Harischandra or Lankadahana; it will end in a holocaust if you play both together on the same stage. Rather, prefer Harischandra and reject the playing with fire. Install Truth in the shrine of your hearts and that will engender the wholesome habit of brotherliness among all men.

BHAKTHI IS ABOVE ALL

Once Narada was asked to name the most noteworthy among the things of the world. He answered that the Earth was the biggest. ; But, he was told water has occupied three-fourths of the Earth; it threatens to swallow up the balance too, bit by bit. So, water, he had to agree, was more powerful. However, water too was drunk up by the sage Agasthya and the oceans were rendered dry by him, and he, in turn, is now just a star in the sky ! Is the sky the biggest, then ? No. For, it was covered by one single foot of the Vamana-avathara of the Lord. And the Lord ? O, He enters the hearts of the devotees and resides there. So, Narada had to conclude that the hearts of Bhakthas are the grandest things in creation !

FAITH CAN COMPEL THE LORD TO MANIFEST HIMSELF

There was a thief who listened quite accidentally to the recital of the charms of Krishna during childhood; he stopped for a moment, but could not pull himself away. He heard the description of the ornaments he wore and got a great desire to rob those precious treasures. He asked the pundit where exactly Krishna would be tending the cows alone or with just his elder brother or with a handful of comrades. The pundit told him rather curtly "In Brindavan, on the Yamuna bank." Planning to catch Krishna alone and deprive him of the ornaments, he hurried off to Brindavan. Sure enough, he met the boy alone next morning at the head of his herd of cows .... but how could he take off the ornaments from that Loveliness ? He was afraid that the removal of even one would reduce the lustre and his heart did not allow him to do that. He looked on for hours, lost in ecstasy, till Krishna himself asked him, but he was too ashamed to mention it. Krishna knew it however. He gave him all the jewels he wore. The thief was overcome with shame and joy; he fell at the boy's feet, but when rose, Krishna was not to be seen. He came to his village and consulted the pundit. "Are these the jewels of Krishna that you extolled the other day " I went to Brindavan and he gave them to me". Needless to add, the pundit fell at the robber's feet. Faith can work wonders; it can compel the Lord to manifest himself and give you what you believe He will give.

GREAT MEN ALWAYS SPREAD THE LIGHT OF THEIR WISDOM

There was a king who led his mighty army across the snowy peaks that bounded his kingdom, into his neighbour's realm. On the lofty pass thick with snow, he saw a mendicant or ascetic sitting on a bare rock, with his head between his knees evidently to protect it from the chilly wind that blew across the gap in the peak. He had no clothes on his body. The king was overcome with pity; he took off his own shawl and coat and offered them to the Yogi (ascetic; one who has mastered the senses and the mind). The Yogi refused to accept them, for he said "God has given enough clothing to guard me against heat and cold. He gives me all that I need. Please give these to some one who is poor". The king was surprised at these words. He asked him where that clothing was. The Yogi replied. "God has himself woven it for me; I am wearing it since birth and will wear it until the grave. Here it is, my skin ! Give this coat and shawl to some mendicant beggar, some poor man". The king smiled, for, who can be poorer than he, thought. He asked him, "But, where can I find a poor man" ? The Yogi asked him, where he was going and why. He said "I am going into the realm of my enemy so that I can add his kingdom to my own". It was the Yogi who smiled now. He said, "If you are not satisfied with the kingdom you have, and if you are prepared to sacrifice your life and lives of these thousands to get a few more square miles of land, certainly, you are much poorer than I. So, offer the clothes to yourself. You need them more than I do". At this the king was greatly ashamed; he realised the futility of fame and fortune and returned to his own capital. Thanking the Yogi for opening his eyes to his innate poverty. He now understood that contentment is the most precious treasure. Great men spread the light of their wisdom through every word and deed of theirs.

CONSEQUENCE OF KEEPING COMPANY WITH THE WILD AND FOOLISH

Once there was a hunter who had captured a baby bear and who brought it up as his pet with great love and care. The bear too reciprocated his love and behaved like a good friend for many years. One day when he was traversing the jungle with his pet, who had grown up into a lusty beast, he felt overcome by sleep, so he laid himself down on the grass asking the bear to see that he is not disturbed. The bear kept watch very vigilantly. It noticed a fly that flew round and round and settled on the nose of the master. The fly went off when it waved its thick heavy hand; but it came again, and settled on the nose. The bear got enraged when repeated waves of the hand did not teach the fly the lesson that his master's nose was not the fly's resting place. At last the bear could not bear the insolence any longer. His heavy palm came down with a thump on the nose, a devastating whack ! The master died on the spot . That is the consequence of keeping company with the wild and the foolish. However affectionate they are, their ignorance will land you into disaster.

THE DISCONTENTED MAN IS AS BAD AS LOST

Resist the temptation to satisfy the senses, to acquire what the world can give, to accumulate material gains set limits to your wants. There was a pupil once, in the kingdom of Raghu, who asked his preceptor at the conclusion of his studies, what dakshina he will accept from him. Dakshina means offering made in gratitude for service rendered. The Guru told him that he needed no other dakshina than his gratitude; it was enough if he lived according to his teachings and brought honour to his preceptor thereby. But the pupil insisted that he must indicate his need and tell him some sum of money of gifts that he would accept. So just to ward him off and get rid of him, the guru named an impossible sum of money; "You learnt sixteen vidyas from me; well, bring me sixteen lakhs of gold nishkas (coins)". At this, the pupil went off, to collect the sum; he went to emperor Raghu, and got from him the promise that he will fulfil his every desire; then he placed his petition for sixteen lakhs of gold nishkas before him. Raghu was rendered desperate by the vast sum needed; though an Emperor, he was too deep in austerity to have the sum on hand, still, in order to keep his plighted word, he invaded the realm of kubera, the God of wealth, and brought back as booty enormous stocks of gold. "Take all this, and give your preceptor what he has asked for; keep the balance for yourself", the king said. But, the pupil refused to take a coin more than what he had to offer as dakshina to his Guru. "I have brought them for you; it is all yours; take", insisted Raghu. But, the young man resisted the temptation and stood his ground. That is real heroism. '*Asanthushtah dwijonashtah*';- the discontented man is as bad as lost. Rely on the lord and accept whatever is your lot. He is in you, with you. He knows best what to give and when. He is full of Prema.

SATHYA (TRUTH) WAS THE SUPPORT OF SHIRDI SAI TOO

I am reminded now of past events, events in my previous body. Even then, I had sathya or truth as my support. A wrestler challenged me then for a fight and he was defeated before a large gathering of villagers. Pained by the insult, he invited Baba for a second tussle the next day, so that he might win back his lost reputation. The man swore that if defeated again, he would wear a long rough kafni and move about with his head covered in clothe. He dared Baba too to swear likewise. Baba was in no mood to enter the arena again and he was quite prepared to concede the fellow the victory he craved. So he accepted defeat and himself donned the Kafni and the Kerchief. The wrestler felt great remorse and his insolence melted away. He appealed to Baba to resume his usual style of dress and released him from the obligation. But Baba stuck to his word. He was Sathya Itself. He wore the new attire.

REVIVAL OF THE VEDAS

Durvasa was a reputed vedic scholar; he had the music of the Samaveda on his tongue and the cinders of Anger in his eye; strange combination, indeed. Seeing this absurdity, Saraswathi, the Goddess of learning and Liberation, laughed in derision. The sage was stung to the quick ; he threw a curse on her and she was born on earth as the daughter of Atreya. There was a brother too, a feeble minded chap, incapable, inspite of the efforts of skilled teachers, of even pronouncing the veda aright. He was beaten with a rod, but that only made him weep helplessly. Saraswathi was moved with great pity. She intervened and saved him from physical torture. She taught him the four vedas and the six sastras and he became a great master.

Meanwhile the Veda had faded from human memory and, as a result, famine stalked the land. Rishis were reduced to skeletons. They yearned for the veda, for that was the sustenance on which they lived. Saraswatha, the brother of Saraswathi, prayed to Chandra or the moon. She made the earth sprout forth edible plants or Saaka, on which the Rishis decided to live. Saraswatha taught them the sixty different sections of the vedas, but so thick was the fog that had descended on the vedas that the sages who learnt the vedas from him were confounded by cynical critics. Narada had to assure them that what they had learnt was the genuine veda itself, but even he could not remove the stain of doubt. They jointly approached Brahma. He said, "You were all able to get this vision of me as a result of your vedic study; you can yourself become Brahma when you practise what you have studied." That was how Saraswatha maharishi revived the vedas once in the past.

RESPECT OR DISRESPECT WHICH OTHERS GIVE HAS NO MEANING

Respect or disrespect which others give has no meaning. These are simply words. There is a small story to illustrate this. In a village, there were two individuals. One of them always used a horse for making his journeys. The second individual would make all his journeys by walking with a pillow on his hand. One day, both of them had to start for the same village at the same time. On that occasion, the man who was accustomed to carry the pillow led the way. Behind him was the person travelling on horseback. On the way, there was another small village through which both these persons passed. The villagers looked at the individual carrying the pillow and thought that he was a peon, carrying the papers, ahead of the master coming behind. They looked at the man on horseback and they thought that he was the officer. In early days, because there were no cars, all the officers used to make their journeys on horseback. That is why the villagers thought that way. As soon as they reached the destination, the man with the pillow went straight into a rest house and sat in a comfortable and boastful manner, resting himself on the pillow. The other was looking round for a place to tie up his horse. The villagers looked at both of them and thought that the man with the pillow was the officer and the man trying to tie up the horses was the peon. This is how respect and disrespect take shape in the world. The person who was thought to be an officer in one village was considered to be a peon in another village. The person who was thought to be a peon in the former village was thought to be the officer in the latter village. This is only imagination on the part of the onlookers and flows from the minds of people. In this process neither respect or disrespect has come to either of them as a result of intrinsic worth.

A STEADY MIND ALONE CAN UNDERSTAND MATTERS RELATING TO THE ATMA

There is a small story with regard to Ramakrishna Paramahamsa. In the midst of giving a discourse, he found a disciple by name Rani Rasamani sitting and pretending to listen to the discourse. He went straight to her and gave the Rani two slaps. Others who were witnessing this event were surprised and were thinking that Ramakrishna did not have a sound mind. Rasamani also was surprised at this and was trying to think if anything was wrong with her and why the Guru was treating her with disrespect. Truly, if one knows one's own faults, he will not commit those faults. In fact, because Rasamani did not know her fault she was not able to realise what was wrong with her. Ramakrishna told her that if she came there to think of her problems of litigation, and not to listen to the discourse, she might as well do so in her house. In the same manner, some people who come and sit here to listen to what is being said here waver and flutter like the leaves of a tree. They move about and look around as if they are crows. They are not able to sit steadily. They look this side and that side. They are unconcerned and unaffected by all that happens here. They cannot even sit properly. Unless you have a steady mind, you cannot understand matters relating to the Atma. They also set a bad example to others. People who have a wavering mind cannot be true yogis, even though they may pass off as good devotees in external appearances.

A SHIRDI EVENT RECALLED

There was a judge who used to come to Shirdi; he asked his wife and child to stay with Baba and left for home for a few days. He said to the boy when he took leave, "This is God Himself". After some days the mother left for Manmad with the boy. There, they fell in with a Kathak who was reciting musically some Puranic story. Within a few minutes, they heard him revile Sai Baba as a mad man and a cheat; the child could not stand it any longer. He tugged at the sari of his mother and forced her to return to Baba.

Next morning, they approached Baba for his blessings and He asked them why they had returned. The incident of the Katha was duly reported. The boy heard every one addressing Baba as the Lord.

Remembering the harsh words of the Kathak, the boy wept, but Baba pacified him humorously, "I am only a man. What the Kathak said is true; I am mad and I am cheating people of what they consider very valuable, but what I feel is useless". Then, even as they were talking, one Mr. Patel came there and related how Baba had saved his child from a serious accident. Baba told him, "Yes, I held him when he fell, with My Four Hands". Patel shed tears of thankfulness; but the Boy cried out, "Ah, I told you, you are God; you have four hands like Vishnu". Baba laughed; He took the boy inside and gave him a vision of Himself, as having Four Hands.

That boy stayed on in Shirdi for 26 years after this and left only after Baba 'left'. He then took sanyas and became a great sage.

NARADA MADE WISER BY THE GOPIS

To conquer egoism, no rigorous system of exercise or breath control is necessary. No, not even complicated scholarship. The Gopikas confirm this truth. They were simple rural folk, untouched by the conclusions of deep study. Narada was once so shocked at their ignorance of the science of spiritual progress that he volunteered to go among them and put them through some lessons in Jnana. He found on entry into Brindavan that the cowherd girls selling milk or curds in the streets forgot to shout the names of their ware but said, "Govinda, Narayana", instead, so immersed were they in God consciousness. They did not know that they had sold off all the milk; they still wandered on, calling out the names of the Lord for the dust of Brindavan was so sacred for them. They had no visaya - vasana, no wish for sensual pleasure; and so, they had no Ajnana. Hence, Narada concluded that they had no need for the lesson he had planned to give. He prayed to them to teach him the means of getting that yearning and that vision of the all-pervading Krishna.

There was a Gopi, for example, called suguna, who had no other thought than those related to Krishna. Now every evening, it was the usual routine in Brindavan for every house-wife to light the lamp from the flame of the lamp at the house of Nanda; they believed that getting light from the flame of the eldest and highest is auspicious. Suguna went with the lamp to Nanda's house and when she reached the house, her mind was lost in the thrill and joy of seeing the very house, where Krishna spent his childhood days, to which his pranks and prattle drew all the cowherd boys and girls. She stood there with her unlighted lamp for a long while, near the big oil lamp illumining the central hall. She was holding the lamp near the flame, but not near enough. She had her finger right over the flame. She not aware that her finger was being scorched by the flame; she was too full of Krishna-consciousness to be aware of the pain. It was Yasoda who saw her plight and woke her from the reverie, or shall we say, vision? For, to her, the house was alive with Krishna wherever her eyes turned. That is the thanmayathwam or identification one must achieve. There is no use if the fledgeling stays in the nest; it should develop wings and fly into the sky. There is no use if man grovels in the dust; he should see the distant goal, clear and grand; he should take to this wings and fly.

FOOD IS THE BASIS OF CHARACTER

There are subtle influences that pass into food from the persons who prepare it and handle it and are absorbed by those who eat it. Food is the basis of character. The state of the mind is conditioned by that of the body. I shall tell you now of an incident that happened eighty years ago. There was a great Yogi, Hamsaraj by name, at Badrinath. He was always immersed in singing the Glory of Lord. He had a disciple who was equally earnest and sincere. That young man was pestered for a few days by a dream which gave him no peace. He saw a fair young girl of sixteen weeping in great agony and calling out pathetically, "Can no one save me ?" The disciple was amazed at this strange dream; he could not shake off that doleful figure and that desperate cry from his mind. He recited his woes to the master. Hamsaraj, I can assure you, was a true Hansa, the Bird of Paradise. The bird can discard water from milk, is it not? Hamsaraj, by his viveka, analysed the situation and discovered the cause of that horrid experience.

He prodded the young man with such questions as; "What did you do the first day? Where did you go ? What did you eat?" etc. It was revealed that he had gone with a friend to a feast and eaten some puris and chapathis. It was discovered that a poor Brahmin had prepared the feast. Well, Hamsaraj sent the disciple to find out why and with what resources that Brahmin arranged the feast for the recluses of Badrinath. The young man cursed the day when the dream started haunting him, for he was now being sent by his master on purposeless errands to investigate irrelevant issues; he wondered how his sadhana could be helped by all this.

Nevertheless, he went and pursued the enquiry about the feast and its origins and the wherewithal out of which it was prepared. It came to light that the funds were supplied by a sixty-year old moneylender to whom a Brahmin had given his daughter in marriage and received in return a sum of ten thousand rupees. She was now appealing to the holy men for a bit of human kindness towards a forsaken child.

Hamsaraj thus demonstrated to his disciple that one should examine the source of the food, the motives for the gift and passions that surge and sway the giver before accepting such an intimate gift as food.

WHEN THE LORD DECIDES ON SOMETHING IT HAS TO HAPPEN

Ambarisha performed a Yaga, but at the crucial moment, the animal intended for the sacrifice escaped. Now the priests ordained that to make amends for this sinful neglect, a human being should to offered as a substitute to the Gods. The King promised 1,000 cows in exchange for a son, but which father will send a son to death, even when 1,000 cows are given in exchange? There were also other conditions; the King's messengers should not ask any one for the son; they should not commit the sin of equating 1,000 cows as equal to a human being; the father too should not break the sad offer to the son; the offer to immolate himself must come unasked from the son, without any prompting or persuasion; it is only such a son that will be accepted by the Gods. Now, Sunasshepa heard the news by himself and approaching his father he said he would go, and gladly too. For, what greater good fortune can a mortal expect than ascending to heaven through the sacrificial flame?

Sunasshepa persuaded his father that his wish to proceed to the Yajna and offer himself was legitimate and approvable, and left for the capital. One the way, he went to his maternal uncle, Viswamitra, who tried to keep away the boy from the sacrifice. "This is all just foolish superstition; can any one substitute a man for a cow?" Viswamitra asked. Sunasshepa replied that all men are cattle, for until Viveka and Vairagya dawn, they are but animals. So, in spite of his uncle's arguments, arguments like the ones used by some to dissuade persons from coming to Puttaparthi, Sunasshepa managed to reach the Yagasala. In the same way as the lights before us are lit when a switch is moved up at Penukonda, when the Lord decides on some thing, it has to happen so. Well, the Lord is not a rock or a stone; His heart melted at the plight of the boy. Indra appeared in the sacrificial fire and departed showering blessing on his head. It was Indra who had carried away the original Cow and elaborated all this plot, to bring Sunasshepa and his greatness to light and to bless him.

ALL NAMES ARE HIS, ALL FORMS ARE HIS

Let me tell you an incident which happened while in the previous body at Shirdi. There was a lady from Pahalgaon, a simple, illiterate devotee. She stored water in her kitchen in three clean, brightly polished brass pots from three separate wells and she had named the pots--Ganga, Yamuna and Saraswathi. She always referred to them by those names. Whenever any thirsty wayfarer called at her door, she mixed water from all three and offered it to the person as Triveni Tirtha. Neighbours used to laugh at her faith, but her belief that the three wells were connected underground with the three rivers that joined at Prayag, was unshakable.

Her husband started on a pilgrimage to Kasi. His mother while blessing his departure, put on his finger her own gold ring and directed him to take good care of it, for it would be a talisman for him. When he was taking the ceremonial bath at the Manikarnika Ghat, the ring slipped into the waters and could not be retrieved. When he returned and related this story, he said, "Ganga wanted it; she took it", just to console his mother. When the wife heard this, she said, "No, no! Mother Ganga will not hanker after the property of a poor old lady. She will accept only what is offered out of love. She will give us back the ring, I am sure. I shall ask Ganga; she is in our kitchen". So saying, she went in and with folded hands, she prayed before the particular pot named by her as Ganga. Putting her hand in it she searched the bottom and ... sure enough, she got the ring back. She had come to Dwarakamayi with her husband and mother-in-law. It is faith that matters; the form and the name on which it is fixed do not matter. For all names are His; all forms are His.

LOVE ALL WHOM THE LORD LOVES

The Gopis had no other Goal, no other Ideal, no other Wish. It was a Surrender of the Self--complete, unquestioned, unwavering. Let me tell you of a devotee, a woman in a small Maharashtra village, who lived in the last century. She went through even the little details of life in this spirit of dedication. Walking was to her a pilgrimage, talking Japam. Even when she threw off a ball of cowdung after applying it over the floor used by her husband to keep his dining plate on while eating, she said and felt "Krishnaarpanam", "May this be an offering to Krishna!" Her Thapas was so sincere that the cowdung reached Krishna and stuck to Krishna's Idol in the village temple every day! The priest saw the mysterious defilement; he was amazed, he was lost in terror; he cursed himself that he had lived to see that sacrilege. Daily, about noon, the same size of cowdung! He hung his head in shame as he walked along, keeping the disturbing phenomenon all to himself. One day he heard that particular lady exclaim "Krishnaarpanam" as she, like many other house-wives, threw the telltale cowdung ball. He suspected; he noted the timings, the quantity, the material etc., until he was convinced that she was the culprit for the disfiguration of Krishna, the defilement of that loveliness. Then he beat her so severely that her arm that threw the dung was fractured.

When he returned triumphantly to the temple expecting to be profusely blessed by the Lord for punishing the wicked woman, he was shocked to find Krishna's right arm fractured and bleeding, exactly like the saint's arm! The poor fellow wept in his agony and said, "I beat her only through love of You; she spoilt Your charm, Oh Lord." Krishna replied, "You must love all whom I love, remember". Here too, I want that you should so behave !...or at least love yourself, that is to say, love your own better self and `best interests'. I will not tolerate envy or malice or hatred among devotees nor will I allow you to hate yourselves or think of yourselves as mean or weak.

IT IS FOOLISH TO IMITATE

Here is a small story. An individual who was living and being educated according to the ancient traditions of India wanted to go abroad for higher education. His father took the son to the goddess and prayed that his son should be kept safe and should return safe to India. The son, seeing the father worship the goddess, also prayed to her in the same way. He was out of India for two years. The boy who had lived in India for 24 years was abroad only for two years. After completing his education, he wrote to his parents that he would be returning home. The parents were overjoyed and met him at the airport. They wanted to take their son to the room where the goddess was and make him offer worship. As soon as the boy alighted from the plane, they noticed that he was in Western clothes. Without bowing to them he asked, "How are you, Mummy?" The mother did not mind it, she was very affectionate and blessed her son. They took him home and he consented to visit the goddess. On entering the main gate, he refused to take off his shoes and became impatient. He thought his parents were uncivilised. While praying, they asked him also to pray to the goddess but he just put his hands in his pockets and refused to do so. When they asked him to do namaskar to the goddess, he asked instead "How are you, mummy?" The father was so annoyed that he slapped his son on the face and said: "You went to the West with the grace of the goddess and after returning home, you have forgotten her. You have become ungrateful and you are not fit to be my son. The traditions you learnt in 24 years have been forgotten by you and the manners and the way of life you learnt in another country in two years are now with you. Will they live with you permanently? It is foolish to imitate. Even ruin is better than to follow another's habits. If we follow our own habits, it will give us joy, happiness and sacredness".

WHICH WATER BAG IS CLEANER?

Because your eyes are directed outward, you will be able to find the faults in others only, but you will not be able to find the fault in your own nature.

Here is a small story. During the summer season, in places round about Nagpur, water will be very scarce. Things might have improved now, but in old days things were very bad. An orthodox old Brahmin lady set out on a pilgrimage. She was so orthodox that she did not touch anything or any one and she did not permit anyone to touch her. She started on a pilgrimage with such an orthodox mentality. By the time she reached Nagpur, she felt that the weather was very hot. She turned on the water taps but not a drop of water came out of them. Her thirst increased. The Government made some arrangement in that station for supply of water. The skin of an animal was used to make a bag. They filled water in such bags and supplied that water to the thirsty people. When several people were drinking the water that was served from that bag of leather, this lady, though she was thirsty, was hesitating in her mind whether the man who was serving the water may belong to a low caste, the bag may not be pure and may not have been cleaned well and so on. She was hesitating to take water. After much hesitation, the lady who could not suppress her thirst, went forward. She questioned the man who was serving the water. "My dear sir, is this bag pure? Is it clear?" The man who was serving the water was clever. He said, "The bag of leather from which water is being served is cleaner than the bag into which that water will be poured after service, namely, your body. This bag is cleaner than your interior." Today we are cultivating this undesirable tendency of looking at the impurity of the bag but not caring to remove the impurity from within our own body.

THE THREE FISHES--SATHWA, RAJA AND TAMA

There were three fishes in a pond. One fish said to the other two, "The water in this pond will run dry day after day. A time will come when the pond may become completely dry and before the fisherman comes to catch us, it is necessary that we go and stay in some place where there is a perennial supply of water". The second fish said: "You are imaging. Your mind is full of needless fears. The pond will not run dry. The fisherman will not come to bother us. Enjoy your present state." The third fish was discouraged when the other two did not accept its advice and so it had to share their fate. As anticipated, the fisherman came and trapped them, cooked and ate them. Our life may be compared to a pond and the length of our life to the water. The three fishes are the three gunas, "tama, raja and sathwa." The sathwic tendency always decides to follow the path of good and fixes its attention on things which are permanent. It decides that before the level of water runs down, it should save itself and it always thinks of noble things. Water has been compared to the length of life and day by day it recedes and at any time death may overcome it. The fisherman is the emblem of death. Tama and raja are antagonistic to sathwa and therefore even the merit of sathwa is counteracted by the other two. These two gunas, tama and raja, mislead our senses and send them along the wrong path. We should first try to control tama and raja and thereby attain mastery over our senses. If we follow good methods even raja and tama may be conquered by close association with sathwa.

A DIVINE EXAMPLE FOR LEADERS

Today people who call themselves leaders are not doing good service and as a consequence, the world around us is becoming very confusing. In this context, a story relating to the Krishnavatara has to be mentioned. One day Krishna approached Yasoda and told her that all his cowherd friends had invited him to go with them and tend the cows and that he was planning to go. The mother explained to him that to go to the forest would mean that he would have to walk on thorns, that he might have to meet snakes and that he might get close to bushes. She said that his tender feet might not be able to put up with the troubles and she said that it would be better if he put on footwear before going to the forest. She said that shoes for him would be ready only the next day and he could go to the forest only the next day. Immediately Krishna asked the mother to tell him how she addressed him. She said that his name was Gopal and that she addressed him by his name. The word Gopal stands for one who tends the cows. He said that he had acquired that name because he could tend the cows and be the leader of the cows. Since the cows would follow him as their leader, he said that he would have to do something which the cows would also do. The cows do not have shoes to protect their feet and therefore he said that he also should not have shoes to protect his feet. He said that he would do only that which persons who follow him could also possibly do. He said that if he wore shoes, the cows would also want to wear shoes, because their leader was wearing shoes. He was not going to wear shoes and allow those whom he had to protect to go without shoes. This is how he argued with his mother. This simply means that when God takes a human form, men will try to imbibe his qualities and will behave like him.

GOD NEVER FAILS THOSE WHO CALL ON HIM WITH FAITH

There was a small temple of Srinath in the town of Govardhana, some centuries ago. A poor Brahmin of that place had an only son, a little boy of six, who was always exulting in the stories and legends of Krishna and who delighted only in listening to the leelas of the Lord. One day, he went out into the meadows with the cattle and when he saw the temple and the image of Krishna inside the shrine, he took it to be the Lord Himself. He called out very piteously asking

Krishna to come out and play with him in the moonlight. Though the doors were locked by the priest as he went out at noon, the Lord came and hand in hand the two walked along the fields in the cool silver light. Krishna had the flute and he sat on a boulder and played on it to the extreme delight of the Brahmin lad. After a few hours, he returned with the friend, whom he called `brother' and, quite unnoticed, He disappeared into the temple shrine, where the idol could be seen through a slit in the door. The boy could not bear the pangs of separation from his Divine playmate; he spent the night and the morning crying outside the door and he was discovered there by his parents and the priest. The parents beat the boy for giving them so much trouble, but, the priest found the idol bleeding, as a result of the blow. If you call on Him as a little brother, He responds and becomes a rollicking playmate for you. Call on Him as a Guru. He will instruct and inspire. He never fails those who call on Him sincerely and in faith.

ONE FALSE STEP

A king once announced that he will honour with a big gift any Brahmin who will agree to do any one of three evil things; (1) He must aver that the Vedas are false, or (2) He must drink liquor, or (3) He must elope with another's wife. For a long time, no one within the seven seas came forward to do anyone of these atrocious things. At last a poor Brahmin on the verge of starvation came into court and offered to drink liquor, an evil which he considered the least reprehensible of the three. But, as soon as he got drunk, he began to swear and curse and in the excitement of intoxication, he shouted in the streets that the Vedas are a tissue of lies; he entered the house of his neighbour and assaulted the lady of the house, like the worst criminal of the land. One thing led to another.

THE SONS

When Jesus Christ entered the precincts of the Temple ofJerusalem, and found people sacrificing doves and birds and other living beings to God, he released the birds and condemned the acts of blood. The priests and scholars resented his act and argued that the God in whom they had faith accepted the sacrifice and was propitiated thereby. They asked him evidence of his authority to interfere with the dictates of religion. Christ went on to tell them a parable. Once there was a farmer who had two sons. He asked his first son to go out to the field so that he may watch the crops ready for harvest. The son refused to obey him. Thereupon, he asked the second son, and he readily agreed. But, what really happened was, the second son later calculated the bother and the sleeplessness which the watching will bring to him; he did not go. The first son later repented for his refusal to do as bidden; he went and watched the crop. Now, Christ asked, who among these two pleases the father more-the son who declared his assent by word of mouth and disobeyed in action or he who disobeyed by word of mouth but obeyed in action? "You may obey in words but disobey in action. My action reveals that I do acts which God commanded. You are your own witness, whether you follow the dictates of the Divine Father. I have greater authority than you, for, your action shows that you disobey whereas my action proves that I follow His commands."

OUT OF THE ROYAL GATE

There was a king called Sathyavratha, in ancient times. He was named so, because Truth was his way of Life, his Goal and his Guide. He derived great joy through the strict adherence to Truth. One day, a few hours before dawn, during Brahmamuhurtha (the time dedicated for meditation on God), he proceeded alone through the Lion Gate of his Fort, in order to have a holy dip in the sea, for the Day was a holy one marked out in the calendar as sacred for such ceremonial baths.

While he was passing through the Gate, he saw a fair maiden with a halo of splendour going out. Curious to know who she was and why she was making her exit at that early hour, he accosted her. She replied that she was the Goddess of Riches, Dhanalakshmi. "I have been long here, now I desire a change. I do not stay in one place long". Sathyavratha told her, "Go! Go! I do not object or obstruct". Presently, a charming masculine figure was seen quietly going out through the Lion Gate. The King asked him who he was and on what errand he was leaving. He replied, "I am Charity; when Dhanalakshmi has left, what do I stay here for?" The King allowed him to leave and he moved on.

Within a few moments, another charming person was going through. The King found that he was Sadachara, representing Goodness in social behaviour. "How can good social relations be sustained without riches and the quality of generosity" he asked. "I am leaving because the two here are no more," he explained. The King agreed; and he moved on. So too, the next emigrant Fame, lamented the departure of the other three and himself wanted to go. The King let him go. He said, "How can Fame survive the absence of Riches, Charity and Happy Social Life?" and the King felt he was right.

Meanwhile, a Person with overwhelming Splendour came into the gate from the Fort, with the intention to leave the City. When asked who he was, he said, "I am

Truth". At this, the King pleaded with him to stay in the City, the Kingdom, the Palace and the Homes of the People. He said that if he leaves, the loss would be irreparable, and life would not be worth while. At this, Truth decided to stay.

And, Fame returned to the Fort in a trice, for Truth is enough basis for Fame to flourish. And, Sadachara returned and grew. So too Charity and Riches came back and established themselves in the Kingdom. All the others were delighted to share the Glory of Sathya (Truth).

VANITY, VANITY!

There was once an old woman in a village. She sold a patch of land that she owned, and with the money, she had four gold bangles made, two for each arm. She wore them with great joy and went along the streets very proud of her new acquisition. But, she was disappointed because no one in the village turned aside and looked at her bangles; she could as well have not worn them, for the villagers did not notice any difference in her. She tried various means to attract their attention towards the bangles, but, without success. One night she could not sleep at all, for, this neglect pained her much. At last, she got a brilliant idea which, she decided, must succeed; the villagers must be drawn to notice the bangles.

Next day, after sunrise, she set fire to her own dwelling house! When the flames rose, and commotion ensued , the villagers rushed towards her, sitting, wailing in front of the burning house. She shook her hands pathetically at the faces of the frightened villagers, causing the bangles to jingle and shine in the red light of the high flames, crying out, "Alas! My house is on fire," "O, pity my fate", "God, don't you see my plight?" Every time she shouted a sentence, she put out her arms vigorously at some one; so that she or he could not miss sighting the bangles. The pity of it! She was so anxious to exhibit her bangles that she did not care for her house itself; the house was on fire but she was happy her bangles were noticed. The scholars who are lost in admiration of their own cleverness are as foolish as this old woman.

COFFEE FOR FISH

You may be compassionate, but, that emotion must be regulated and wise. A compassionate man once brought home a fish he found struggling on the bank of a river in full flood; he placed it between the folds of the warm blanket and poured hot coffee down its throat. He thought it was suffering from a fit of cold. The hot coffee killed the poor thing. He could have saved it by throwing it back into the floods. He lacked the intelligence which would tell him what to do to express his compassion.

WHEN THE GODS TEST A MAN

Sibi was a genuine Sadhak, having attained a high stage in detachment and the spirit of renunciation. The Gods decided to discover whether his achievements were deep-rooted and unshakable.

Agni (the God of Fire) and Indra (the God of the Heavenly Regions) took on the forms of a dove and hawk. The hawk (Indra) pursued the Dove (Agni) across the sky, until the frightened bird fell into the lap of Sibi sitting on his throne, pleading for protection from the hawk. As befitted his Dharma, Sibi gave word that he would save the dove from its enemy and assured full protection for it. At that moment, the hawk presented itself before the Emperor and demanded its meal, its legitimate prey. "I am hungry, I had secured my food; you have deprived me of my meal", it complained. "Of what use is all your vaunted spirituality if you rob me of my meal?", it lamented.

At this, Sibi said, "Yes, I shall slice off flesh from my body weighing as much as this dove weighs; you can appease your hunger with that." The hawk agreed. A balance was brought; the dove was placed on one pan, pieces of flesh cut from the body of Sibi were placed in the other pan. But, lo and behold, however many pieces of flesh were laid thereon, the pan on which the dove sat did not rise at all. It was indeed a mystery how the bird weighed so heavy. At last, Sibi said, "Well, You can take all of me. Eat me whole. Here I am at your disposal".

No sooner did he utter those words than the hawk became Indra and the dove was transformed into Agni--Gods effulgent in their Glory! They were supremely happy at the depth of Sibi's spirit of renunciation; they blessed him profusely and departed.

SHE WAS HIS TEACHER

There was a rich man once who owned a rice mill. He heard a Pundit expound that the Service that God appreciates most is the gift of food to the hungry. So, he decided to serve food to the poor in his village. But he had no mind to use good varieties of rice for the purpose. He felt that any rice is good enough for them. So, he got the rice that was rotting in his godown--he did not care even to remove the worms that infested it; he cooked it and served it to the hungry poor, who ate it and suffered many illnesses as a consequence. His wife expostulated with him and told him that good food given to 10 persons would be more meritorious than bad food given to hundreds! But he was in no mood to listen to sound advice.

The wife therefore hit upon a plan to teach him. She placed on his plate every day food that was rotten and full of worms. When he grew angry and castigated her, she replied, "The Pundit said that every one has to suffer for the injury he causes others; you have to eat, in the other world, rotten food, full of worms. I am giving that type of food to you even now, so that you may get used to it. It will help you to eat the consequence of your evil deed". At this, the husband realised his iniquity; he repented for his wrongs and learnt better ways of service to the poor.

THE FIRST SLIP

A mother used to carry her son on her shoulder, when she went to the market. A woman with a basket of fruits passed by her; the child lifted a banana from that basket and started eating it. The mother noticed it, and when she was told that he had cleverly lifted it from the basket of a passing fruit seller, she complemented the son on his smartness. This made the child indulge in petty thieving and picking pockets, as it grew into a boy--and in actual housebreaking and dacoity. Once during a dacoity, he committed even murder, and when he was caught and jailed, he expressed a wish to see his mother before being hanged. The wailing, weeping desperate mother was brought before him. She was sobbing at her son's fate. The son asked her to come closer to him; suddenly, he tried to strangle her, and the guards separated them. The son said, "She deserves the punishment; for, it was she who brought me to this doom. Had she reprimanded me when I stole a banana when I was a child of two years, instead of complementing me, I would not have fallen into this evil way".

INDIANS TAUGHT ALEXANDER

There is a story of Alexander the Great, which illustrates the glory of Indian Culture. It seems Alexander used to go incognito to the villages around his camp, in India, in order to learn the habits and manners of the strange new land into which fate had brought him. One day, he found a man pleading with another to accept a pot of gold, which the other was refusing even to look at! He came to know that the pot of gold was discovered under the soil of the field purchased by the man from the man who refused to accept it. The buyer argued that he had bought only the land and was therefore not entitled to own the pot of gold; the seller said he had no right to any thing found on or in the plot that he had sold. Alexander watched this contest for some time; both did not yield At last, the village elders were called in to decide the issue. And, even as Alexander watched, the elders found a happy way out; the buyer's son shall marry the seller's daughter, and the pot of gold shall be given to the bride as dowry! Alexander felt elated at the heights to which human virtue could rise; he was also ashamed at his own adventurous ambition to conquer another's property by force of arms. The ideals underlying the ancient culture of India have to be studied and practised by every Indian at least, so that the world might have the benefit of the great example this can provide.

WHO WROTE IT?

Once a District Educational Officer was inspecting a school. He asked the teacher to find out from one of his pupils as to who wrote the Ramayana. The pupil innocently replied, "Sir, I never wrote it; perhaps you might have written it". Then the teacher found himself in a miserable plight and turned to the Inspecting Officer to assure him that he had not done so and tried to enquire if the officer had by chance written the work. The District Educational Officer referred the matter, to be safe, to the Vice-Chancellor, who finally observed that some Brahmin must have done it and advised the officer concerned to close the issue. This means that the state of affairs in our educational field today is so pitiable that our students, teachers, inspecting officers and Vice-Chancellors are all sailing in the same boat. Nobody knows about the author of a work like Ramayana. In these circumstances we are not justified in calling ourselves educated.

THE KALINGA EPISODE

Among all the wondrous adventures that astounded people during Krishna's childhood, revealing the Divinity that had come among them, the Kalinga episode is the most meaningful. The serpent Kalinga was poisoning the waters of the Yamuna and the atmosphere over it with its breath; all who approached that area, men or cattle, fell dead. But, Krishna--the Divine Boy--jumped into the depths, forced the foul snake to rise above the level of the river, and leaping on its hoods, danced upon them with His tender lotus feet. The pressure of those soft silken soles was enough to force the deadly poison out from the fangs of the monstrous cobra and render it harmless for ever. This is a great lesson for man. This leela is quite unlike earlier incidents which evidenced the Child's super-human strength and wisdom. He was lifted away by the storm-demon, he was hit by the calf-demon, he was felled by the cart-demon, he was pecked at by the stork-demon, he was poisoned by the nurse-demon; but sceptics can easily ascribe these miracles to accident or coincidence or exaggeration. But, the Kalinga episode is a parable, it is a valuable lesson in spiritual sadhana.

WHAT ACTIONS PLEASE GOD

We must experience only the eternal bliss with the Jiva and not the worldly things. We must perform good actions with the body and must have good promptings by the mind. It is only such things that please God and draw forth His Grace.

Here is a small example. There is a big wall-clock. There are three hands on it. One is a second hand, another is a minute hand and the third one is the hour hand. The second hand travels very fast, moving round the 12 numbers in 60 seconds, while, during this time, the minute hand moves through only the little mark or division. After the minute hand travels through sixty divisions, the hour hand moves through one hour. Sixty seconds make one minute and sixty minutes make one hour. Because the second hand and the minute hand travel relatively fast, we are able to see their motion. Because the hour hand travels slowly, we are not able to see its movement. In the same way, after we perform a number of good deeds, the mind reaches a good place; when the mind thinks of a number of good thoughts, the Jiva reaches the holy place of Atma. We are able to see the body-acts reaching the Jiva, but not the acts of the Jiva reaching the Atma. Our body is like the second hand. Our mind is like the minute hand. Our life is like the hour hand. Therefore, we must do a number of good deeds through our body. We must contemplate over many good things with our mind. Only then, can we reach the holy place in the Jiva thatwa. These are called the gross, the subtle and causal states. When we want to reach the causal stage, we must do many good things with this gross body and contemplate many good things with the subtle mind.

RAMA BLESSES GOVARDHANA HILL

Nothing ever happens without proper cause, however, accidental or mysterious it might appear. The roots go deep and are out of sight. I was telling Hislop, in Bombay, at Dharmakshetra, the same thing. The bridge towards Lanka was being built over the straits, so that Rama and His army could march across to the realm of the demon King, Ravana, where Sita was interned. The valiant monkeys were plucking mountains and leaping vast distances in space with those peaks hoisted on their shoulders, so that they could be thrown into the sea to create a passage for Rama! The monkeys had formed a queue all the way from the Himalayas down to the southern most point, where the bridge was fast coming up. When the causeway was completed, word went fast along the queue that no more hills are needed and each monkey placed on the ground, wherever it stood, the hill it had on its shoulder at the time.

One hill, however, did not sit quietly. It started bewailing its fate! "Why was I removed from where I was and why am I now refused? Alas! I was elated that I am destined to server a Divine Purpose; I was overjoyed that the Armies of Rama and Rama Himself will walk over me. Now, I am neither there, nor where I was!" It shed profuse tears. News reached Rama, and His Compassion was great. He sent word that in His next Avathar, when He will come again upon His Mission in human Form, He will certainly bless the sorrowing hill. This was the Govardhana Peak which the Lord (as the boy Krishna) lifted on His finger and held aloft for full seven days, in order to save the cowherds of Gokul from the Deluge of Rain that Indra dared to inflict on them!

STRAIGHT DEALINGS-ALWAYS BEST

Those who are too weak or unsteady to go through the prescribed discipline bring all kinds of lame excuses, when charged with malingering. A farmer's dog was a fierce animal; it leaped towards a visitor with bared teeth and would have bitten him, but for his timely discovery of a thorny stick on the ground, with which he hit the dog on the head. The dog retreated howling in pain: the master heard it and got wild at the visitor for inflicting wounds on the dog's head; he dragged him to the Royal Court. The king asked him why he had beaten the dog which according to the farmer was quite a harmless pet. The visitor said that it had actually leaped at him and bared its teeth. The farmer said that this did not justify his using a thorny stick; he could have used a smooth stick instead. The visitor reported that when one is anxious about saving his life which is in jeopardy, one has no time to discriminate and pick and choose; he has to use what his hands find. Besides, he asked, "Why, the dog could have threatened to bite me with its tail; when it bites with the teeth, I have to reply with something equally sharp". The Raja appreciated his point and he was acquitted. Because it was his pet, the farmer resorted to all these tactics; the visitor had to use counter tactics. Straight dealing could have avoided the bother.

"IS THAT REAL" OR "IS THIS REAL"?

Reality can be grasped in a flash of illumination, as happened to Emperor Janaka. One evening, Janaka was in his Durbar Hall, surrounded by his courtiers and a bevy of female musicians; they sang sweet melodies and the Emperor enjoyed the music so well that he slept off, while on the throne. No one had the temerity to wake him; they all quietly slipped into the inner apartment, lest their talk and movements might disturb him. He was left alone with an attendant, and the queen. At about, midnight he screamed pitiably and awoke at the sound his queen ran towards him: the Emperor asked her, "Is that real?" She could not find an answer to this question, for how could she know which was that and which was this? The Emperor asked every one the same question; in fact he spoke no other word. That question was continuously on his lips. News spread that Janaka had gone mad; there was mourning everywhere. A sage who heard of this came to the Palace and was brought to the Imperial Presence. He assured Janaka that he would answer his question, provided he told him what he saw in his dream, while sleeping on the throne and why he screamed so.

Janaka had a dream. He dreamt that rival kings had joined forces and invaded his dominion and captured his capital and that, to save himself from them he ran into a forest. Fleeing from his foes, he had no food for days together. He was too exhausted to move. But, hunger dragged him on. When he came to the outskrits of a tribal village, he saw a man washing his plate after taking food; he shouted to him asking for a few particles. The man gave him a small morsel, but, as bad luck would have it, a crow flew in at that moment and snatched it away! That was the reason why screamed in agony.

That was why he asked, "Is that real? Or, is this real?" The hunger was as real as the throne; ruling over the Empire is as real as the loss of empire was in the dream. The sage told him. "That is unreal; this too unreal. That was a Swapna, this is Jagrath, both are Mithya (not false, because they are relatively real;

though not absolutely real they have temporary reality, a reality that is negatived by subsequent investigation and experience). But, you dreamed, you woke, you screamed, you asked; therefore, you existed during both stages; so you alone are real". The "I" that persists in all the three stages-waking, dream and deep sleep-that "I" is the only reality; it is the "I" that appears as all this manifested Universe.

HOW FAR IS VAIKUNTA?

Provided your intellect is sharp and free from prejudices and predilections, the reality will reveal itself to you in a flash, for it is quite a simple thing. Only, it must be capable of seeing the problem in its basic essence, apart from all the jumble irrelevancies. Once a very learned Pundit was holding forth in a very pedantic manner the story of Gajendramoksha from the Bhagavatha, before the Maharaja in his Durbar Hall, before a large gathering of courtiers. He described how the Lord, on hearing the agonised call for succour from the elephant held by the jaws of the monstrous crocodile, hurried from Heaven(Vaikunta) without stopping even to collect His insignia and weapons, without even intimating to His Consort where He was bound to and on what mission. Suddenly the Maharaja interrupted him with the question. "Tell me, Pundit, how far is this Vaikunta?" The learned Pundit did not know the distance; he was non-plussed. Nor did any of the other scholars in the Palace know.

But the servant who was fanning the King from behind the throne offered to furnish the answer, if his impertinence be pardoned. The Pundit was shocked at his effrontery, but the Maharaja allowed him to speak. "Your Majesty! Vaikunta is as far as the cry of the elephant could be heard", he said. Yes; when the anguish of a devotee's heart is expressed as a cry or a groan or a sigh, the Lord is as far only as that sound could reach; He is always on the alert to listen to the cry of His children. His Residence, Vaikunta, is within hearing distance of every cry, from every grief-stricken heart. That illiterate servant knew in flash the Omnipresence and the Compassion of the Lord.

CULTIVATE DIVINE QUALITIES

Man must reveal the divine qualities of love, humility, detachment and contentment; if he does not, he becomes worse than a beast and more deadly. There was a dog that pleaded with Rama for a place in the aerial car in which he returned to Ayodhya. When Rama asked the reason for this strange behaviour and request, it said that man had become worse than worms and fleas; he had started tormenting dogs who were loyally serving him.

One should so live that no pain is caused to other beings through one's activities. And, one should be ever grateful for kindness received. Karthaveerya was treated with lavish hospitality by Jamadagni, but the wicked man coveted the Kamadhenu that made the lavishness possible. Bharthruhari, on the death of the queen, was so struck with remorse that he wept and moaned on the cremation ground itself, for days on end. Seeing his inconsolable plight, one sage came before him, with a mud pot in his hand. Right in front of the bereaved man, the pot slipped from his hand, fell on the hard ground and was broken. The sage wept and moaned and was inconsolable. Bharthruhari consoled him and said, the broken pot cannot be made whole by any amount of lamentation. Suddenly he realised the absurdity of his own behaviour and stopped crying; this was the purpose of the sage's ruse !

You come to Parthi, listen these discourses, nod approval and clap hands in appreciation. But when you pass through the gate on the way home, it all evaporates. Or, you apply the lessons you learn in an indiscriminate way and suffer. There was a merchant who used to attend discourses and when he heard a speaker say that cows should not be driven off while they are feeding, he looked on, when a cow entered his shop and ate off a good portion of the grains he had kept for sale. Later, he was told that he should not take every bit advice he received as valid for all occasions; and he advised his son, "Look here, you sit on the floor on a towel while listening to the discourse, is it not? When the discourse is over and you rise up, do you not wave the towel forcibly in the wind to shake of all the sand it collected? Shake off from your mind and brain all the ideas and advice you have collected during the discourse and then, come home." If you do as that merchant advised, what is the benefit of coming, staying, hearing and being exhorted?

A SUPER THIEF

When you attempt to deceive another, remember there will emerge some who can deceive even you. There was a thief once who was skilled in all the stratagems and tricks of that profession. There was not a single one that he had not mastered. One day, after collecting a large number of costly articles and bundling them up, he was moving along a lonely road with the booty on his shoulder. He saw a child standing on the bank of a wayside tank, weeping aloud, in great distress. The thief went near and asked, "Why are you weeping? What has happened to you?" The child said, (and here, you have to remember that it does not matter how old or how young a person is; it is the intelligence that matters). "I came here for a bath; my golden necklace fell into the waters, right there, where I tried to have a dip The place is too deep for me." The thief thought that he could get away with this necklace too, for it was a little child that stood between him and the jewel. So, placing his bundle on the bank, he went down into the waters to retrieve the necklace. Meanwhile, the child lifted the thief's bundle and running a short distance, disappeared into the jungle.

The thief came up disappointed, for the necklace was but a fiction, only to find that he had been robbed! Whoever deceives another will have some one cleverer to outwit him.

TWO MINUTES OF THE FORBIDDEN FRUIT

There was a famous dacoit once who advised his son while initiating him into the ancestral profession, never for a moment to listen to stories of the Lord. "Do not stay to listen to any Purana or any reading of the Bhagavatha," he exhorted the young aspirant. The son scrupulously observed this injunction for years and amassed a good fortune. One night, however, while running with his loot on his shoulder through a side lane of the city to avoid the police, a piece of glass cut his sole: he sat for a while to pull it off and stop the flow of blood. He was then behind a house, where some one was reading and explaining the Bhagavatha to a small group of listeners; he listened perforce for a short two minutes. The spark fell on the heap of cotton. During that short period, he heard the pundit explaining the nature of God. He has no ears, no eyes, no limbs: he has a thousand forms; He is without form. Sarvathah paani-paadam," as the Gita says. That description got fixed in his heart. He could not shake it off.

A few days later the police came to know of the depredations made by him as well as his associates and Kinsmen. In order to know more about their activities they entered the area incognito one constable as Kali and some others as the worshippers and priests. They shouted and yelled, cursed and terrified the dacoits and called upon them to come out of their homes and fall at the feet of Kali.

Many did so, but the son who had heard the Bhagavatha, albeit for two minutes, knew just enough to save his skin. He was not terrified at all. He challenged the constable who was acting the role of Kali and tore off his make-up and exposed the plot and instilled courage into hearts of the gang. Then, when the police left discomfited he argued within himself thus; "If two minutes of the forbidden fruit could help me so much, what can I not gain, if I devote myself entirely to the stories of the glories of God?" He left off the evil path and became a Sadhaka.

WHERE IS GOD ?

Once upon a time, a monk wearing the ochre robe chanced to enter a village full of atheists; he fell in with a gang of defiant youth who challenged him to show them that the god whom he was adoring actually existed. He said, he can; but before doing so, he asked for a cup of milk.

When the milk was placed before him, he did not drink it; but, sat looking at it, long and silently, with increasing curiosity. The youths became impatient; their clamour became insistent. The monk told them ; "Wait a minute. I am told that there is butter in milk ; but, I must say this cup does not have it, for, I do not see any of it, however hard I look into it !" The fellows laughed at his innocence and said "Silly man ! Don't rush into such absurd conclusions. Milk has butter in every drop; that is what makes it so nourishing. If you must see it as a separate concrete entity, you have to boil the milk, cool it, add sour curd, wait for some hours for it to curdle, then, churn it and roll the butter that floats into a ball". "Ah", said the monk, "that makes my task of showing you god much easier ! God is in everything , being, atom of the universe; it is because of this that they exist and we can cognise them and enjoy them. To see him as a concrete entity, you have to follow a prescribed procedure, earnestly, strictly and sincerely. Then, at the end of it all, you can experience his grace and his glory."

GIVE UP AT LEAST ONE BAD HABIT

A wicked man once went to a Guru for initiation into spiritual life. The Guru asked him to give up at least one of his bad habits; he gave up uttering falsehood. That night, when he went to the royal palace to commit theft, he found on the terrace another person, who said, he too was a thief. He too announced that he was a thief and both broke into the treasury and divided among themselves the diamonds found there. The other person was none other than the king; he pretended to be a thief and he knew where the keys of the treasury were ! While the diamonds were shared, the honest thief felt pity for the king of the realm who was losing his entire stock; he asked his companion to leave one diamond behind, in the safe. And, it was done.

Next morning, when it was discovered that the treasury was looted, the minister was sent by the king (who had acted as thief the previous night) to assess the loss. The minister found a diamond that had missed the eyes of the thieves. He quietly transferred it to his own pocket and reported at court that all the diamonds were gone !

The king had got from the honest thief his address the previous night while they parted company, with their separate bags. So he sent for him and when he stood in court before the king , he confessed that all but one of the diamonds were stolen by him and his unknown associate. The diamond was discovered in the pocket of the minister and the king dismissed him for the lie. The honest thief was appointed minister instead, and he gave up his other evil habits too and pleased his guru, by his fame as a virtuous administrator.

GOD TESTS AND REWARDS

The Pandavas celebrated the Aswamedha yaga, and as part of that ceremony released the chosen horse so that it may take its own course across the length and breadth of the land. Whoever stops and binds the horse is thereby challenging the sacrificant for a fight; he has to win back the horse, after defeating the audacious obstructionist.

Mayuradhwaja, a great devotee of Krishna, a virtuous ruler, a wise man learned in the Vedas, a man of deep compassion, held the horse, and Arjuna, the Pandava Hero, decided to meet him in battle. But, Krishna advised him to desist ; for, he desired to demonstrate to Arjuna the devotion of Mayuradhwaja which far surpassed his own; he also desired to proclaim to the whole world the heights that Mayuradhwaja could reach in the realm of self-sacrifice and truthfulness. So, he proposed that he and Arjuna proceed to Mayuradhwaja's palace in the guise of a pair of Brahmins, seeking a meal. They were welcomed by the king, who offered them rich hospitality. But, before they could eat the very first mouthful, Krishna stopped very dramatically and recited a tale of woe.

"Listen ! O Soft-hearted Emperor ! As we were coming along through a forest on the border of your empire, a tiger snatched away the young son of my companion here. Before we could come up with the beast, it had swallowed half the body; but, it heard our piteous appeal, and promised to release the boy, and return him alive to us, provided it is given as substitute, one half of the sanctifying body of the pure and holy emperor of the land, Mayuradhwaja. How can we relish your hospitality with this agony in our hearts ? Promise to give the tiger half your body in exchange for the full living body of this Brahmin boy, and then, we shall partake of your hospitality". Mayuradhwaja agreed most gladly; when the lunch was over, he sat on the floor and instructed his queen and his son to saw his body into halves.

They placed the saw on the head and began the process of division, with the Brahmins witnessing the operation. Drops appeared in the left eye of the king. Krishna said, "O ! You are giving us the promised gift with tears, not with unalloyed willingness. I cannot accept anything given with tears." But Mayuradhwaja replied, "Sir! If I am unwilling or hesitating, both eyes should shed tears, shouldn't they? Only the left eye is shedding them now; and the reason is this : the right half is being used for a highly sacred purpose, to save a person from cruel death. But what will happen to the left half? Cast away, to be eaten by dogs and vultures? So, the left half is weeping, but, the right half is jubilant that it is being put to some meritorious purpose". At that moment, Krishna manifested Himself to the great Mayuradhwaja in all His Glory and Majesty; He blessed him that he would have Krishna always installed in his heart and that he would be ever blissful and content. Arjuna too realised that there were devotees of Krishna far more advanced than he was. His pride was humbled. Mayuradhwaja's humility was rewarded.

Tests such as these are evidence of Grace rather than of Anger. The terrible aspect of God is not terrible in essence. God is described in the scriptural texts as, "Raso vai sah", He is sweetness Itself. How can sweetness ever become bitter?

THE DEVOTEE RAN AWAY

A clever villager used to enter the village temple in the early hours of the day and sit on, with eyes closed, in the hope that people will honour him as a great devotee. Since he did not get up and go about his business until about mid noon, the temple priest was hard put to it to close the doors and go home for his daily tasks there. So he struck upon a plan to stop the nuisance. He knew that the closed-eye session of Dhyana was all a pretence. He hid himself behind the Idol of Deity, and when the villager was well set in his pretence of deep meditation, he said, in an imposing sonorous voice, "Listen! Excellent Devotee! I am mightily pleased by your asceticism and your steadfastness. Come I shall merge you into Myself." At this, the fellow ran fast out from the temple, leaving no trace of where he had gone to!

The devotion and sense of surrender of men are similar to those of this imposter. Faith is weak, discipline is absent; earnestness is lacking.

DHARMA PAYS

The armies gathered by the Kauravas from their kingdom and from their allies were standing face to face with the forces of their Pandava cousins. Cavalry, elephantry, and infantry, eager to start the destruction of the enemy, the chief Actors all accoutred and equipped for the fray! Conches were blown; trumpets rent the sky with their blare. The air was tense with hope, fear, anxiety and anger. Blood in million bodies became redder and warmer; hearts pounded quicker: arms grasped weapons in deadly grip.

Dharmaja, the eldest of the Pandava Brothers, suddenly, removed his footwear; he laid aside his armour; he slid from his chariot; he walked towards the opposing cohorts, towards Bhishma, the Generalissimo of the enemy forces. Duryodhana, the eldest of the Kaurava Brothers, the cousin most responsible for the war, the unyielding opponent of the Pandavas, saw Dharmaja cross over to the aged Bhishma. He was overjoyed; he guessed that Dharmaja had decided on surrender for he was by nature against bloodshed and battles.

The four brothers of Dharmaja were astounded. Bhishma, the redoubtable hero of a hundred contests with the Kauravas, the person most eager for the battle to begin, felt foiled of victory. He recalled the many occasions when Dharmaja had stood in the way of revengeful action against the Kauravas. He feared that he would apologise and withdraw like a craven from the bloody gamble of war. Arjuna the formidable bowman, witnessed his brother's defection with horror and anger. Nakula and Sahadeva, the twins, were struck dumb at their helplessness.

Lord Krishna studied the situation from the seat of the charioteer on the chariot of Arjuna, which was in the front line of the Pandava army. He signed to the four them to follow their eldest brother and do likewise.

He said, "All these years you have revered him, and trod on his footsteps. Do so now. Do not hesitate; do not doubt." Dharmaja was the very embodiment of Dharma, he knew the right and he practised it whatever the consequences. He knew that Dharma will guard those who follow Dharma. He never did a hypocritical or a non-Vedic act; he never took a wrong step. He went straight to Bhishma and fell at his feet. Standing before him with folded hands and bowed head, he prayed, "Grandfather! We had no chance to experience the love of the father; he passed away soon. You brought us up from infancy with love and care, and made us what we are today. We have no right to fight against you; but, fate has conspired to bring us now into battle with you. Please have mercy on us; permit us to raise our arms against you"

Bhishma was naturally charmed and overjoyed at the humility and righteousness of Dharmaja; his eyes were filled with tears at the strange turn that distiny had taken; he blessed him and said, `Dharmaja! You have stuck to Dharma in spite of the temptations this situation has placed before you. What a noble example you have set before the world! This Dharma that you follow will itself give you victory"

Next, Dharmaja and the brothers moved towards General Drona, the Brahmin Preceptor, who had taught archery to both the Kauravas and their cousins, the Pandavas. Dharmaja fell at his feet too and prayed "Highly revered Preceptor! We five are your pupils; how can we rightfully take up arms against our Preceptor? The times have indeed gone awry. Pardon us for this wrong. Permit us to engage with you in battle". Drona the Acharya, was visibly moved by this appeal. "Ah! How great and good, this Dharmaja is ! Even at this moment when the hounds of war are to be let loose to spread death and fury, he is sticking to the dictates of Dharma!" Drona was thrilled at the thought. He clasped Dharmaja in his arms and said "Son! You are dearer to me than Aswathaama, for I am drawn to him only by duty, whereas I am drawn to you by love. You are all my sons, for, I love you as such. Your Right will certainly earn victory over might.

It is this adherence to Dharma that ensured their victory.

SLOTH

Shower Ananda on others; lead them along the godly way; be an example in sincerity and earnestness. Partake in Bhajan and Namasankirtan; have share in the singing, loudly and with enthusiasm. Some ask me, "Why should we sing aloud? Isn't it enough if we feel it in the silence of the mind?" This is mere dry Vedanta! They are prepared to advise others in the Samithi, but, are unwilling to practise the advice themselves! Two friends were remarkable for their sloth; one of them had to catch a train at 3 A.M. So, he asked his friend to wake him up at 2-30 A.M. for he had no faith himself. The friend was even more of a sloth! He wanted that he should be awakened by his friend at 2-15 A.M. so that he could wake the same fellow at 2-30! How can anything be accomplished by such men?

LESSON FROM SIVA

Siva is the supreme exemplar of serenity! Siva according to the Puranas, has a curious assortment of family members. Yet, each one is so calm and without agitation, that the Divine Family exists in peace and concord. Siva has snakes on His arms, round His neck, on His head, around His waist! One of His sons, Kumara rides on a peacock, which attacks snakes; another rides on a mouse, which the snakes feed on! One son has the head of the elephant, which whets the appetite of the Lion, which is the vehicle used by Durga, the Consort of Siva, who is so inseparable that she is the left half of the body of Siva Himself. Nor is the Lion friendly by nature to the Bull, which the Lord Siva Himself has as His vehicle!

Siva has fire on the Central Point of His Brow, and Water (the river Ganga) on His head--incompatible both! Imagine how loving, how cooperative the various components have to be to render life on Kailas smooth and happy!

It all depends on the mind and its proper discipline. The weapon of Love will disarm every opponent. Love begets Love. It will be reflected back, it will have only Love as reaction. Shout `Love'; the echo from the other person's heart will also be `Love'.

THE WINNING SMILE

Once it happened that Krishna, Balaram and Satyaki who were quite little boys at that time, scarce four or five years old, strayed into a thick jungle, all alone, when darkness fell, and there was no way of reaching Gokulam! Of course, as you must have guessed already, it was a stratagem of Krishna; even at that age, he would do nothing without a deep purpose behind it and the purpose would invariably be teaching some one some good lesson. They decided to spend the night, just where they were; Krishna put fright into them with his descriptions of ghosts, ghouls and demons roaming in search of human prey. He proposed that two shall sleep for three hours at a stretch while the other one kept watch.

It was Krishna's duty to keep awake and be on the lookout from 7 to 10; Satyaki was to be vigilant from 10 to 1 A.M. and Balarama was to start his part of the duty at 1 and keep on till 4. Satyaki sat up at 10 and Balarama and Krishna laid themselves on beds of dried leaves and slept soundly. Meanwhile a demon did actually present himself before the little Satyaki. He fell upon the boy, who resisted heroically, dealing and receiving hammer- strokes with fists with a good number of clawing and biting in between. The demon had to retreat at last, leaving Satyaki badly mauled, but happy. The two brothers were sound asleep; they had not been disturbed in the least by noise of the encounter. Satyaki had met blow with blow, and dealt injury for injury. At 1, he awakened Balarama and stretched his body on the heap of leaves, as if nothing had happened. The demon invited Balarama too for combat and had to retreat humiliated, because Balarama too was a fierce as he, and his blows were even more terrible than Satyaki's. Balarama too curled himself into the bed at 4 A.M., after waking up Krishna who was to keep watch in Brahma-muhurta, the auspicious hour when Gods are to be propitiated, that is, until dawn.

The demon came roaring like a wounded tiger, and advanced ferociously at the little Divine Boy. Krishna turned his sweet charming face at him, and rewarded him with a lovely smile. That smile disarmed the demon; the longer he came under its influence, the weaker became his vengeance and venom. At last, the demon became as docile as a lamb; when the other two woke, they were surprised at the victory that Krishna had won by the weapon of Love. You cannot destroy anger by anger, cruelty by cruelty, hatred by hatred. Anger can be subdued only by forbearance; cruelty can be overcome only by non-violence, hatred yields only to charity and compassion

SENSE OF DUTY SAVED HIM

Bhishma was a mighty warrior; he was famous for the grandeur and glory that he won, through both detachment and Divine Grace. In the vicinity of his kingdom, Bhishma once had to encounter a person called Chakradhara. This man had undergone severe austerity and received from God as a reward for pleasing Him, an invincible discus (Chakra- wheel) so people hailed him as Chakradhara, the wielder of the Divine Wheel-weapon! The fellow had become so insolent and wicked that he wrote a most insulting missive to Bhishma, on the death of Shantanu, Bhishma's father. Chakradhara wrote, "Either send the widowed queen to my palace zenana or meet me in battle"! Who could tolerate such insults and keep quiet? It is said that everyone has to guard Dharani (land), Dharma (faith) and Dharmapathni (wife). Bhishma said to himself. "What is my life worth if I cannot avenge this insult, if I cannot save my mother's honour?" But, the Brahmins of the court advised him that he should engage himself in combat with Chakradhara, only after ten days; for, during the ten-day-period after the death of his father, he had ceremonial pollution and during that period, he should not handle the divine missiles he had with him. He could not utter then, the holy mantras which can activise them. "Finish the religious rites to appease the departed soul of your father and then, destroy the foe in battle", they advised. Bhishma realised the propriety of their counsel and sent a message to Chakradhara, inviting him for the fray ten days later!

But, Chakradhara could not delay that long: he was itching for victory; he directed his newly won weapon at Bhishma! But, a wonderful thing happened! That Chakra which had come from the hand of God would not harm a son who was doing his scriptural duty, performing the Vedic rites for the manes! It rotated in the sky for ten days, waiting for the funeral-pollution period to end! When one is devoted to his duty, one is surrounded by such powerful protecting influences that no injurious force dare approach. That is the way Grace operates. Personal skill when reinforced by Divine Grace can work wonders, as happened when the horde of monkeys successfully built a bridge across the sea to Lanka.

HE HAS NEITHER

There is the story of a young man who was riding a cycle on a dark night along a crowded road; the policeman on duty asked him to stop and alight, for, he had no lamp on his cycle. The fellow, however, shouted, "Policeman! Keep away. Of course, I have no lamp; but, beware. I have no brake, either!" That is the pathetic condition of every one now. No one has the lamp of wisdom, or the brake of sense-control. How then can they go along the road to Ananda, without causing injury to themselves or others? The cyclist must have both; man too has need of wisdom and self-control. Or else, he is certain to ruin this chance he has got, to save himself.

GOD WITHIN

When you speak with the tongue or see with the eye, or plan with the brain, who is it that speaks, sees, judges and decides? It is the One Intelligence, the One that, like a current works in and through all men and materials, God. When you are immersed in Bhajan, note who the One is activating you! Your tongue pronounces the words in the tune designed for them; your palms beat the time; slow or fast; your head sways in unison with the sentiments that the words express; your mind is gushing Ananda, at the magnificance of the pictures that the song evokes. So too, a dancer is articulating harmony and melody through every gesture and movement of muscle and limb. But, all the activity originates from a common source, God, who is resident as President in the heart. When he is ignored, neglected, or denied, there is no joy for you or through you for other. You are either Thamasic--dull, inert, or Rajasic, passionate, fanatic, but not Sathwic--pure, balanced, serene!

God is All. He is all Forms, His are all Names. There is no place where He is not; no moment when He is not! (Even the Devil has the syllable Dev, to indicate his affinity). Thunder is God's message; the rain is His Grace. Let no second pass without awareness of God; let no event lapse without reminding you that He is the artificier! You have an image or picture in the room you have set apart for worshipping God. You light a lamp before it! You say, 'I have lit the lamp'; but, is it you really? Who endowed the oil, the wick, and the lamp, the property of producing a flame together? Who moved you to revere the picture in this form? Who was it that placed the lamp, lit it and bowed before the picture? It is all God, God, God. There is none else, nothing else, for the man who knows and feels.

COMMON SALT OR COWDUNG

You may be a master of the Gita and the Bhagavatha; you may claim to have spent decades in the service of Krishna; but, without the Key of Love you cannot gain entrance to the Go-loka where He resides! You may be in Prasanthi Nilayam since years, claiming to be with Swami and near Him; but, without cultivating Love expressed in Service you cannot know Me.

There was a pupil once, who prided himself on his ancestors and his master; they were great pundits renowned over the entire realm. His preceptor asked him one day whether he could answer any question he might ask. The pupil was stung to the quick! He said, "Why this hesitation? Ask, and it will be answered! I come from a Somayaji family; my father is a celebrated savant. I have been learning at your feet for years! Don't I know the answers to all questions you might ask?" The teacher wanted the answer to the question, "What is the meaning of the word, Lavana?" The pupil laughed and said, "O, you surprise me, with this absurd question! Don't I know? Lavana means--cowdung!" Well; lavana is a word that is in daily currency in every household and everyone knows, it means `common salt'! Even this, the conceited disciple had not learnt. Unless you brighten your vision with Love, you cannot see the Truth.

NARA AND NARAKA

The most widely current among the legends on Deepavali refers to the demon Naraka whom Lord Krishna, accompanied by His Consort, Sathyabhama or Sathya, destroyed in battle, this day. Naraka was the son of Mother Earth, of Bhoomatha. She asked for a boon from the Lord that the Day should be observed in his memory, as a Day of Light or Joy and the sharing of Joy by one and all. Therefore, hundreds of tiny lamps are lit this evening and kept in rows before and within every home in India; but, few are the lamps that are lit in the cavity of the heart to destroy the darkness that lies thick within.

Who exactly is this Naraka, the demon Narakaasura, let us inquire. He is described as tyrant, who had no reverence towards elders and saints, who was afflicted with a severe type of land hunger, who looted and plundered unchecked, who carried away princesses and damsels by the hundred and threw into prison without any compunction, and who never repented for any of his crimes and sins. When the good men of the world appealed to Lord Krishna for succour, He invaded his kingdom, laid siege to his capital City, and overwhelming his forces, allowed His Queen, Sathya, to slay him on the battlefield.

This legend has profound undercurrent of meaning, which you should not miss. Naraka is an asura, a demonic person. His City is named, Praag-jyothisha-pura; praag means, the previous; jyothi, means light; and sha means, forgetting or ignoring. So the City's name means: The city of those who have laid aside the previous light. That is to say, the City of those who are ignorant of Atmic Splendour. No wonder they are demons. No wonder they are lustful, full of hatred, greed, envy and egotism. They had become so lost in their sins that Lord Krishna did not vouchsafe to give them the honour of being killed by His Hands. He directed Sathya to destroy them. Yes. Ignorance so fundamental and so deep can be destroyed only by the sword of Sathya or Truth.

Egoism is of earth, earthy; not of heaven, heavenly. So, Naraka is the son of Earth. And, he is called Naraka, Nara means, man who knows his manas (mind), who practises manana (discriminating reflection on what he has heard and what he has been taught). But Naraka which means hell is the name appropriate to one who believes he is the body and toils to cater to its needs and its clamour. When man grows in physical strength, economic power, mental alacrity, intellectual scholarship and political authority and does not grow in spiritual riches, he becomes a danger to society and a calamity to himself. He is a Naraka to his neighbours and his kin. He sees only the many, not the One; he is drawn by the scintillating manifold into the downward path of perdition. A-suras have another name in Sanskrit-Nakthancharas, those who move about in the dark. This is a fair description of their pathetic condition. They have no light to guide them; they do not recognise they are in the dark; they do not call out for light; they are unaware of the Light. Their intellect has become the bonded slave of their passions and their senses, instead of establishing itself as their master. When at last, Truth appears before them and overwhelms them, they recognise the one and merge happily in it.

The lamp is not merely the symbol of the knowledge of Truth. It is also the symbol of the One, the Atma that shines in and through all this multiplicity. Just as with one lamp, a thousand lamps can be lit, and the One is as bright as ever in spite of the thousands deriving light from it, so too, the Atma illumines the Jivas (individual selves) and shines in and through them, without undergoing any diminution in its splendour. The Atma is the Cause; all else are effects.

Naraka sought to act freely as his emotions and passions dictated. The Upanishads call upon man to roam about in the jungle of life as the King of Beasts, the Lion, and not as panic-stricken cowardly sheep, ashamed to lift its head. Face the six foes that are ferociously gnawing the heart of man, lust, anger, attachment, pride, hatred, greed, and be MEN, Nara, not Naraka, who cringes before these foes and tries to propitiate them by yielding to their demands.

TWO SIRENS

There are two evil sirens that entice youth into futility and frivolity, diverting them along the paths of ruin. One of them is called, Dame Cinema and the other is named. Dame Novel. The film contaminates and corrupts; it pollutes young and innocent minds; it teaches crime, violence and greed; it destroys the basic humanness and degrades it into bestiality. Even ochre-robed monks are steadily dragged down to sin by its insidious influence.

Dame Novel too corrupts equally, with salacious pictures of bestiality. They both lead the young away into the wilderness of vice. They do not know, nor do they care to know, how to shape the young into self-reliant, self-confident, self-knowing citizens.

NO LIFELINE

There was a student once who held out his palm before a palmist for scrutiny. The palmist examined the lines with care and announced that he would advance very much in education. The student was very happy. He predicted that he would amass large sums of money; the student's joy knew no bounds. He declared that the lines indicated fame along with fortune. This filled the cup of joy to the brim; it could hold no more. Then, the palmist announced that the `lifeline' was short and it ended abruptly, quite quick! The student fell in a faint.

Education too has no lifeline now; it does not ensure the skills and attitudes essential to live a life of peace and contentment.

GRAMMAR AND GRACE

When Sankara was residing at Varanasi (Benaras City) on the Ganga with his pupils he used to visit the pundits in their own houses, and draw them into beneficial conversation on themes of philosophy. One day, when he went to a pundit, he found him immersed in complicated rules of grammar. When asked why he had taken the intensive study of grammar, he replied that it would easily fetch him a few pieces of silver. "If I am designated as a Pundit, I can go to the home of some big Zamindars, and hope to receive alms and offering from them, for the upkeep of my large family", he said. Sankara advised him in appropriate terms, and charged him with self-confidence and courage.

Returning to his hermitage, Sankara wrote a verse summarising the advice he gave to the poor struggling Brahmin householder: *Bhaja Govindam, Bhaja Govindam, Bhaja Govindam, Moodha Mathe, Sampraapthe Sannihithe Kaale Nahi Nahi Rakshathi 'Dukrn karane'*

"Praise God, Praise God, Praise God, you fool. When death does knock at your door, rules of grammar cannot save you."

Sankara exhorted his pupils to disseminate the ideal of this verse, and they too, responded with verses on the same lines, each of the 14 contributing one verse. Sankara added another twelve of his own, as well as four more verses about the transformation that the teaching would confer. Thus there are 31 verses in all, in the text called Bhaja Govindam or Moha Mudgaram. The latter name means, "The weapon with which delusion can be destroyed". Each one is a step in the ladder which raises man into God.

Sankara addressed these verses to "moodha mathi", "the foolish person". Now, who are these fools? He has given the answer in another context: 'Nasthiko moodha uchyathe'. Those who deny the Atma are fools". Those who assert and believe that "I am not this perishable body. I am not this feeble intellect; I am undying everlasting all-inclusive Atma" are few indeed. The vast assert and believe that "I am the moulder of my destiny. I am the captain of my ship. I choose my likes and dislikes. I fulfil my desires through my own efforts". These are the fools.

THE BANDAGE ON THE NOSE

There was once a Sadhaka who approached Guru for guidance. The Guru gave him an idol of Vishnu and also necessary instructions for daily worship. But the Sadhaka found that, even after some months of meticulous Puja, he did not get any spiritual reward or elation. So, he reported his dissatisfaction and the Guru gave him another idol, this time of Siva and asked him to have another try. The disciple came after another six months demanding another idol, because even Siva had failed him. This time, he got a Durga idol, which he duly installed in his domestic shrine. The two previous idols were standing, dust ridden and neglected, on the window sill. One day, while Durga-Puja was going on, the disciple found that the perfumed smoke from the incense stick was being wafted by the breeze towards the idol of Siva on the window sill. He got wild that the ungrateful stone-hearted God who was deaf to his powerful entreaties should get the perfume intended for his latest idol! So he took a piece of cloth and tied it round the face of Siva, closing up the nostrils that were inhaling the perfume.

Just at that moment, to his immense surprise, Siva appeared in His splendour and Glory before the Sadhaka! The man was dumbfounded. He did not know how the ill-treatment had induced Siva to give him Darsan. But what had really happened? The Sadhaka for the first time believed that the Siva idol was alive, conscious, chaitanya-full and it was that belief which forced him to tie the bandage on the nose. The moment he realised that the idol was full of Chith, he got the Realisation he was struggling for.

THE DESIRE TO DIE

There was a woodcutter once, going daily into the forest and collecting a bundle of fuel which he sold in the village nearby for a pittance, which just sufficed to keep his wife and children alive. One morning, while he was stepping out of his hut, the wife reminded him that it was Yugadi (the New Year Festival) the next day; she pleaded with him to collect a heavier bundle of fuel that day, so that they could get a few more paise to give the children a morsel of sweet rice each. The man nodded assent and walked on. He succeeded in gathering an extra huge bundle; but, with that heavy load on his head, he was soon exhausted; he had to deposit it on the ground, before he could approach the village. This set him thinking of his plight. He had lost all his old zest for living. He called upon the Angel of Death, the Mrthyudevatha, to relieve him. He cried, "O Death! Have you no mercy toward me? Why have you forgotten me, so long? How I wish I could die and escape from this daily grind!" The Angel of Death took pity on him, and appeared before him, to fulfil his wish. But, the woodcutter suddenly receded, he cleverly changed the purpose of his appeal to the Angel. He had no wish to die, though in his despair, he had called for her help. He said, "No. No. I have no one here to lift this bundle on to my head, so I called on you to come to my aid. That was the only reason behind my prayer. Please help me to lift this burden and place it on my head; I have to reach the village soon ! Since man is innately immortal, he recoils from the grasp of death; the will to live is very strong, much more persistent than the will to die.

THE NON-EXISTENT ENEMY

The Sun-God was, one day, very much impressed by the 1008 names which a devotee offered Him worship. He listened to the Names as he uttered them in steadfast faith. He was particularly alerted when he called upon Him as Andhakaradweshi--He who was looked upon as the enemy of Darkness. He could not tolerate the existence of an enemy alive; so, He called for a war unto death on this Demon called Darkness. He went into all the places where Darkness hid himself; but, no sooner did He spot him, the demon disappeared so that He could never come to grips with him. Finally, He concluded that Darkness was non-existent and was only a creation of the imagination of His adorers! Before the Splendour of Immortality, the darkness of mortality too would flee in haste.

The resident in the body has no birth and therefore, no death. But, man is hugging the falsehood that he is the body and so is subject to death and birth. A silver cup can be reshaped by the smith into a plate, or later, into a pan-box; but though the name, the form and the function vary it remains the same.

SAND INTO GOLD

There is a story connected with the construction of the great temple at Kalahasthi. It was built according to tradition by sage Agasthya, helped by Bharadwaja. Every day when the sun was about to set, Agasthya called every worker before him as he sat on the river bed and under his instruction, two sages poured into the lap of each worker sand taken from the bed; that was his wages! Now, that sand changed into gold in strict proportion to the work that the receiver had put in that day. If one did more work, he got more gold; if less, less. If one had wasted the entire day, it would remain sand, so far as that worker was concerned.

There was no injustice, no grumbling, no favouritism. All worked in the presence of the All-seeing and, all accepted the gold that was vouchsafed by the Almighty, for it was just his due no more, no less.

It is work that is done in this spirit, the spirit of the constant presence of the Lord, that is honest. The Lord will reward by His Grace the work that is done sincerely and gladly, not work that is done for fear of superior officers. If hearts are pure your work too would be pure.

WASTE OF TIME

There was a doctor in Benares who spent 5 minutes in the morning and 5 in the evening for meditation on God. Knowing this, his colleagues and friends laughed at the idiosyncrasy. One day they argued that he was wasting ten precious minutes on something which he had been misled into believing. The doctor replied, "Well, if God does not exist, I agree that I am wasting ten minutes a day. But, what if He exists? I am afraid you are wasting your entire lifetime. I prefer to waste ten minutes rather than a lifetime. Why should you grudge me the ten-minutes-joy that I derive there-from? I am not robbing you of your joy; why should you rob me of mine?" He asked. The cynics were silenced.

HE YELLED THE TRUTH

There was once a famous scholar who earned great fame as a Vedic exponent, but no one could guess his caste. Many suspected that he was not a Brahmin, but there was no means of discovering. At last, the wife of a Pundit said she could easily solve the problem. The scholar was invited for a feast at the place and when he was fast asleep after a full repast, she applied to the sole of his foot a red-hot brand at which the Vedic scholar yelled "Allah". Thus it was discovered he was a Muslim. Faith should not be a matter of exposition; it should be patent even when you yell in pain.

BROKEN POT

There was a man once who hired an aged elephant for the bridal procession on the occasion of the marriage of his daughter. After the ceremony, when the procession returned home, the bride descended from the howdah and at that very moment, the elephant crumpled and died. The owner of the elephant was shocked at the news; he refused to take it as an unavoidable misfortune. He insisted that the identical animal had to be returned to him alive. He went to court on this issue. The judge had some mud pots kept at the back of the door which the greedy owner had to open for passing through. When he opened it, the whole lot was broken. The judge insisted that he had to restore those very pots! Thus was sense driven into that fellow's brain.

EVEN GODS MUST OBEY

You must have heard many stories of Garvabhangam, the suppression of conceit or egoism by the Lord. One day, Anjaneya appeared in a garden on the outskirts of Dwaraka. Krishna who heard about the pranks of the strange monkey, directed Garuda to proceed and scare the animal out of the city limits. Garuda failed, even though he took the entire army with him for the fray. His pride was humbled. Krishna sent a message through him to the monkey, who had declared himself as Anjaneya, that he should deign to come to Krishna's Court. But Anjeneya recognised only Rama and he would obey only the orders of Rama. So, Krishna had to send another message that Rama was calling him to his audience hall! Devotion compels the Lord to yield to the whims of His servants. Anjaneya hurried to see Rama; Krishna gave him the Darsana of Rama Himself!

THE BEGGING BOWL

When a child dies, ask yourself the question, "Is it for my sake that he was born?" He had his own destiny to fulfil, his own history to work out. Gautama Buddha's father was so overcome with grief when he saw his son with a begging bowl in the street that he told him thus: "Every one of my ancestors was a King; what misfortune is this that a beggar was born in this line?" Buddha replied, "Every one of my ancestors had a beggar's bowl; I know of no king in my line." The father and the son walked different paths, travelled along divergent routes.

OH! I HAVE DIED

There was a father-in-law who was so angry with the son-in-law for not writing letters to him and his daughter from foreign lands where he had gone as a soldier, that he wrote to him an angry letter: "You are as bad as dead, so far as we are concerned, for you do not care for your wife any longer. So she has shaved her head and started wearing widow's weeds". The soldier, when he received this letter, lamented aloud that his wife had become a widow, not realising that so long as he was alive, that calamity cannot happen!

Do not jump to conclusions, abdicating your discrimination. Don't deny the validity of your own experience. Stand on your strength. Be unmoved, either by adulation, or denigration.

RAMA'S CHEEK

There was a merchant who was exhorted by his teacher to repeat the Name of the Lord; he pleaded he had no time to sit and repeat it; the shop took up all his time and energy. He had to go a little away from the village every morning for answering calls of nature. He spent about half an hour for this. So, the Guru asked him to use this time for the daily Smarana. Hanuman, the great Ramabhaktha, was passing through the sky, when he saw the merchant defecating and heard him repeat `Ram Ram Ram' while so engaged. Hanuman was incensed at his impertinence, he was desecrating the Name by pronouncing it while unclean. So, he gave him a hard blow on the cheek and continued his journey to Ayodhya.

When he reached the Divine Presence and looked at the splendour-filled face of Rama, he noticed the swollen red print, of a hand upon His Cheek. Hanuman was shocked and His grief was too deep for words. Rama told him, "Hanuman! Do not ask Me the name of the person who dealt this blow. I always dissipate the moment of a calamity for my Bhaktha and I intercede in time to save them. That poor merchant, sitting outside the village, who was repeating My Name when you were coming here, could he withstand the terrible onslaught of your angry palm? The fellow would have collapsed on the spot. So, I intercepted the blow and received it on my own cheek, my dear Hanuman."

FINE OR GHEE

A merchant was once hauled up before a magistrate for selling adulterated ghee which smelt bad and was a danger to health. Judgement was pronounced that he should either himself consume the entire quantity of ghee as a punishment, receive 23 strips, or pay a fine of 100 varahas. He preferred the ghee and started drinking the stuff, but finding the smell unbearable, he chose the stripes. He received about a dozen but he could not stand more. So, he finally told the magistrate that he be let off with the fine. If only he had opted for it first, he could have avoided the foul drink and the excruciating pain. By his indecision, he had to taste the reek and the rod.

THE CLEVER OLD WOMAN

There was an old woman who had two grand daughters, one a termagant and the other a modest girl. When they touched her feet before departure from her house, she blessed them thus: the termagant she blessed, "May the festoons and the auspicious Rangavalli drawings on your doorstep be ever fresh and untrodden, unwiped; may your purse be full, ever undisturbed". She meant, of course, to curse her with barrenness. The other girl, she blessed thus, "May your doorstep be unclean, may your purse be emptying fast" meaning that she would have a number of happy boisterous children; a mode of blessing for a married woman, usually given by grandmother. On the face of it, this looks like a curse and the other statement a blessing. But, the inner meaning is different. This grannie blessed unasked; the modest and truthful person can also receive blessings out of the spontaneous Grace of the Lord, provided he is steady in his virtues.

NEGLECTING GOD

There was a king who sought a teacher who could put him into heaven; he was so conceited and drunk with power that he felt he deserved it. When any one came forward, he plied him with such impossible questions that they were aghast at his impertinence; but the king did not leave them at that. He threw them into prison. At last, one man came promising to show him the way. He was brought into court and seated before the king. The man, however, took no notice of the king, but began conversing with the courtiers and the pages and attendants, inquiring after their health and wishing them well. The king was incensed at this neglect of his high authority and he asked the soldiers to lead him out and give him a thorough beating. The man said, "Before I am led out, let me tell you this : I am to be given a thorough beating because I did not respect you first, but bypassed you and talked to these servants of yours. Well, God is the king of kings, the Lord of all the Worlds; you have neglected Him; you are bypassing Him; you talk only to these servants; consider what punishment you deserve for this". The King realised his blunder and thanked the teacher for removing the veil of conceit.

TWO LETTERS REMAINED

There is a story in the classics to illustrate the worth of the name Rama. Sage Prachetas once composed a text with verses numbering hundred crores! The three worlds competed among themselves to take the entire text; the struggle assumed calamitous proportions and so God brought them together and persuaded them to accept a third each, that is to say, each world (Heaven, earth and the Underworld) received Thirty three crores, thirty three lakhs, thirty three thousand and three hundred thirty three verses each; one verse remained undivided. It had thirty-two syllables in all; so, when it too was allotted among three co-sharers, at the rate of ten syllables each, two syllables were left over. How could two be divided among three? So, God decided that they be adored and received by all three worlds equally--the syllables were `Ra' and `Ma', making up the priceless key to salvation: Rama!

HIS OWN ROCK

There was a monk near Haridwar who had given up for many years both hearth and home and was living on alms; he used to heap all the food he collected on a flat rock that jutted out of the Ganga and used it as a plate from which he took his meal. One day, he came to his rock and found another monk sitting there, taking food! He got enraged at this trespass on his `property'. Then the newcomer said, "Alas! You have renounced all sense of I and mine; you have shaved your head, so that you may not be recognised by erstwhile companions; you yearn to be free from all bonds; but, you have tied yourself up with this rock! How can you swim across this Sea of Samsara with this Rock round your neck? You are leading a life of hypocrisy". That opened his eyes to the error.

THE REPENTANT DOG

When Sri Rama decided to end His Avathar career and walked into the flooded Sarayu river, a dog too followed the concourse. When asked why it had attached itself to the entourage, it said, "I desire to enter Heaven with you all. I was, in my previous life, a full-fledged Yogi; but I slipped and fell from the straight path of self-control, I became the slave of conceit: I expounded the Vedas as my fancy dictated, in strange but attractive ways; so, I have now become this animal that takes delight in barking, biting and baying. The persons who encouraged me then by praise, are now the fleas and flies that crowd on my skin and pester me. Help me Lord, to escape from this disgrace; I have worked out my Karma; I have lived out my sentence". That is the consequence of irreverence shown to the Vedas; study them reverentially and with a view to practise what they teach. Desisting from practice is itself irreverence.

RUKMINI'S MARRIAGE

Rukminikalyana is not simply the story of a marriage. It is the union of Purusha with Prakrithi itself. The Brahmin intermediary is the symbol of Vedic authority through which alone the merging of the two is known. Rukmini is the Jiva and Krishna is the Paramatma. She is suffering from the rules and restrictions imposed by Prakrithi. Ahamkara is her brother, worldliness is her father. But on account of her Sadaachaara, her mind rested on God. So she was able to plan a method of reaching God. Her prayers, repentance, yearning and steadfastness were rewarded. Her observance of the age-old code of good conduct at last saved her; for, she went out for the Gouri Puja before the marriage rite. In that temple she was immersed in the worship of God and so she was liberated from the bonds by the God who was lying in wait! The parents and the brother and all the relatives objected; but, an individual is born to work out one's destiny, not to live out one's days according to the plans laid down for one by others, however dear or near they may be.

THIS WILL NOT LAST

The senses are the villains, they instil the delusion that you are the Upadhi. Curb them as the bull is curbed by the nose-ring, the horse by the bit in the mouth, the elephant by the goad. When the Pandavas were traversing the Himalayas towards the end of their careers, Dharmaraja was still affected by mental anxieties and so he prayed to Krishna to spend some time with them. On His departure from their dwelling, Krishna gave Dharmaraja a note, which he was to read to himself whenever he was affected by joy or grief. The note read "Eppudoo undathu" (It will not last for ever), that is one method by which mental agitations can be calmed.

HIS DHARMA CHANGES

Man is journeying through the stream of life from one act to another; it is continuous activity, marked by Karma throughout. There was a consummate actor who went to the Darbar of a king in the role of Sanyasin. The king honoured him as a great monk and asked him various questions on sadhana and philosophy which he answered using profound vocabulary and appropriate terms. The king was very pleased and he ordered his minister to bring a plate of gold coins as offering to the saint. The sanyasin spurned the gift. He said that as a sarvasangaparithyagi, one who has renounced all attachment and desire, he cannot even glance at it and left in a huff. The next day, the same actor came to the palace as a female dancer, very orthodox and restrained. The king appreciated it highly and the minister brought forth the plateful of gold coins. The dancer refused to accept it, because it was too small a recompense for the skill exhibited. The king suspected from the voice that it was the sanyasin of the day previous that was standing before him as the female artiste. Finding that his surmise was correct, he asked him why he was asking for more today when he had refused to take the same gift the previous day. The actor replied , "Yesterday, I was a sanyasin and so, it was my Dharma to refuse; today I am a dancer and so it is my Dharma to earn as much remuneration as I can from my fans".

THE WISER WIFE

A husband may not be aware of the excellence of his wife's spiritual attainments. There is the case of a couple who were proceeding through a thick jungle on pilgrimage to an inaccessible shrine. The husband saw on the footpath a precious stone, shining brilliantly when the sun's rays fell upon it from between leaves. He hastily threw some sand over it with a movement of his foot so that his wife may not be tempted to pick it up and became a slave to the tinsel. The wife saw the gesture and chided the husband for still retaining in his mind a distinction between sand and diamond. For her, both were the same.

RETURNED WITH THANKS

Buddha was seated alone one day, and later, some men gathered around him. One among them who did not like his teachings and the effect it had on the people, got up and started a tirade in very vulgar terms against him. Buddha sat smiling listening to all that calumny, without a single gesture of disapproval. The man got frothy in the mouth through rage, his vocabulary was fast getting exhausted, his tongue began to show signs of overwork, but, Buddha only asked him with a smile ; "Brother, have you finished"? The man said, "You have no sense of shame ; you do not even react when I abuse you. You are thick-skinned; you are a log of wood". Buddha asked him, "If a person does not accept a gift, what happens to it ?" He said, "It remains with the giver". "Well, keep these gifts of abusive words with you, brother ! I do not accept and react".

THE DAUGHTER-IN-LAW'S DICTUM

There was a beggar who once wailed before a rich man's house for a mouthful; the master, reclining in an easy chair, drove him with harsh abuse. But, the beggar persisted. He asked for some stale food, at least! At this, the daughter-in-law who was at her meals in the inner apartments replied: ``My dear fellow! We are at present eating stale food. The fresh dishes are now being cooked". The beggar knew what she meant; he understood that the woman was pointing out that the father-in-law by his insolence and cruelty was preparing for a miserable future, while his present high standard of living was made possible by the merit he acquired through charity in previous lives! We eat stale food, that is to say, the result of the acts in past lives. We are also cooking our future meals.

MAALADASA

There was a cowherd called Maaladasa who was determined to see the Lord as He was described in the sacred texts he had heard expounded in the village temple by a pundit. So he prayed and prayed to the "Dark Lord riding on the white bird" all the time his cows were pasturing in the fields. Eleven days passed; but there was no sign of the "Dark Lord riding on the white bird". He had forgotten to take food and drink during all those days and so, had become weak, too weak to walk or talk. At least, the Lord melted at his entreaties and presented Himself before him as an old Brahmin; but the Brahmin was not riding a white bird, nor was he dark, beautifully dark, as the Pundit had described. So, he asked the Brahmin to come the next day at seven in the morning, so that he may bring the pundit and verify whether He was the Lord Himself.

The Pundit laughed at the whole affair and refused to take part in it; but, Maaladasa was so importunate that he agreed. The entire village turned out on the river bank the next day, long before seven o'clock. The Brahmin was there, exactly as he had promised and Maaladasa showed him to all. But, they could not see him ! They began to laugh at the cowherd's antics and threatened him with severe beating for bringing them all along as butts for his joke. Maaladasa could see the Brahmin clearly but no one else could. At last, he got so enraged that he walked upto the old Brahmin and gave him a whacking blow on the cheek, saying, "Why don't you show yourself to all ?"

That blow changed the entire scene. The Brahmin disappeared. Krishna appeared in resplendent robes, smiling face, captivating form, and the white bird. As the astounded villagers were recovering from the amazement, a Heavenly Chariot, the Vimana, floated down from the sky and Krishna asked Maaladasa to sit inside it. Then with the Lord by his side Maaladasa rose up and soon was out of sight.

BABY'S INVITATION

Krishna was only a few weeks old when a certain ascetic came into the house of Nanda; Yasoda was having the baby in her lap. Of course this is an incident not found in any book; I have Myself to tell you this. The maids ran in, for, they were afraid the child might start weeping at the sight of the uncouth figure. He walked in nevertheless, and Yasoda found that when he was sent away, the baby raised a cry, not when he was approaching. The Muni also announced himself as having come to see Krishnaparamatma, a name that was new to the entire family. No wonder the baby cried when that distinguished visitor was asked to go! Devaki had been given the vision of Krishna being the Lord himself, but this Muni had discovered the arrival of the Avathar, by the Grace of the Almighty. It was the Baby who had invited the Muni for His Darsan.

SUGUNA

Then, there was Suguna, another gopi. One day, when Krishna was with Sathyabhama, He pretended to have severe stomach ache and in spite of all the remedies that she tried she would not afford relief. Ofcourse, it was all acting, superb acting, such as the paralytic stroke I had for a week previous to Guru Pournami recently!Even Rukmini was not admitted into the house by her to inquire about Krishna's health. But, Rukmini found Suguna pining outside the door in great agony at the illness of the Lord. She gave her the articles and asked her to go in. Krishna welcomed Suguna and made her sit at His Feet and ate the fruits she had picked up from Sathyabhama's own garden and suddenly, the ache had gone. It was her agony at the Lord's condition, her simple sincere devotion that was so effective. There should be no artificiality in your attachment to the Lord, no affectation, no pride, no egoism left, to soil the freshness of the flower you offer. Sathyabhama protested when Krishna accepted the fruits, for, Krishna had brushed it aside as tasteless when she had herself offered them as the precious product of her assiduous gardening effort. They were tasteless, since her pride had entered into it; now, when the simple rustic Gopi picked them from the ground and saturated them with her devotion, they became tasty and attractive, for the Lord cares for the Bhava not the Bahya!

In the Kuchela episode, the wife of Kuchela plays a more important role than Kuchela himself. She has much more Bhakthi; in fact, women are more devotional than men. They can master their minds better. It was her maternal love that prompted her to send Kuchela to the Lord so that her children might get a full meal. She had faith in the Lord. Kuchela hesitated and argued that Krishna might not recognise him or invite him in or accept his homage.

FOLLOW THE WISE MAN

Some people were on one bank of a river and since they were strangers they sought information whether the river could be crossed at that point and how. A lame fellow said, "It is dangerous to cross at this point; go further down". They did not believe him, for he could not have waded through! A blind man said, "You can cross; only, keep more to the left for some distance and move to the right afterwards". They did not follow his advice, for he could not have known; he must have been led by some one else. At last a man came, who volunteered to take them across. "I have crossed often; I live on the other bank and I own lands on this side". So, they followed him with confidence and they could reach the other bank safe.

THE THORN ON THE ROAD

A young man got married one morning, at 9 o'clock. In the evening the newly wedded couple left for a walk. On the first day wedded life, the mind of the young man was engrossed in the welfare of his wife. They walked side by side. The young man saw a thorn on the way. He did not want his wife to tread over it. So he pulled his wife away from the thorn well in time. Six months went by. While they were walking again, he saw another thorn on the way. In a very casual manner, the husband said: "There is a thorn in your way; try and avoid it." He was not as anxious as he was on the first day of their wedded life. One whole year went by. They were walking to some place again and he saw a thorn on the way. His wife was walking without noticing. He angrily reprimanded his wife saying: "There is a thorn. Are you blind? Can you not see?" Notice how within one year, the love of a husband to his wife has undergone transformation.

THE GURU SPOKE

One day, when Naren was in his room, at night, sleepless because he was tossed about by conflicting thoughts Ramakrishna who was 'asleep', was talking as if in a dream, but his talk was clearly heard by Vivekananda. He said, "O Manas! O Maanasarajahamsa! O Nithyaanandarasanilaya. You are Daivaswarupa. Sport in the pure lake of Dhyana of the Divine. Instead, why do you crave for the dirty pond of sensual pleasure!" That was the advice of the Guru to Naren. Naren immediately resolved to take that advice to heart.

THE TENDER FEET

The influence of the Divine is such that while you are contemplating it, all trace of envy and greed will disappear from the mind. The boy Krishna had entered a Gopi's house and was just standing beneath the milk-pot hung above when she discovered Him; Krishna ran out into the street and the Gopi pursued Him, and wanted to catch Him. She wanted to catch Him soon, for she was so pained that the boy was running in the hot sun. She never worried about the loss of curds or milk or butter, but, the thought of Krishna's tender feet walking over the hard stones in the sun was something she would not bear.

THE BANGLES ON THE HAND

Uddalaka, a contemporary of Chaithanya, chose to worship the Lord as the Manifested, as prakrithi. The Creator he chose to worship through his creation; he adored the Container for the thing contained. In short, he adored Radha, or Dhara in reverse, the Prakrithi aspect, the Feminine principle, as Krishna, the Purusha, the inseparable Other! His yearning was so moving, his Thapas was so compelling that one day, while a Bangle-seller was trudging along the bank of the Saraswathi River by the side of the village, he found a damsel washing clothes in the bathing Ghat. The Lord is as anxious to assuage your pain as you are anxious to secure his Grace to get rid of it. You may not know this, but I know, for I feel it. She called him near and selecting many pairs of bangles, she wore them all. At last, when he asked for the cash, she said, "O, I forgot all about the money that is due to you, please go to the house of Uddalaka in the village; any one will point it out you. Ask him; tell him that his daughter purchased them and he will surely pay. Or, wait, you may tell him that he will find the cash behind the picture of Radha in his shrine room".

The man took her at her word and hurried to the village and the house of her parents. Uddalaka was amazed at the tale for he had no children. In fact, he had not even married. But the bangle seller insisted on his looking behind the picture of Radha because he said the girl was incapable of decoit. Uddalaka denied having ever placed any cash there. How could he use that space of all places for keeping cash? But just to satisfy the bangle- seller, he peeped there and, lo, he got a knotted piece of cloth containing just the cash needed to pay for the bangles. Then, in a flash, he realised that it must be Radha herself who had sent the man and he fell at the feet of the pedlar and ran with him to the bathing ghat, overcome with joy and thankfulness. For an instant he saw a glorious vision above the waters; the right arm of Radha, with the bangles scintillating in the morning sun. He knew the arm was raised to bless him; he felt it was calling him, he flew out of the mortal coil into her Lap.

THE CRY THAT CAN SAVE

There is a fine story about Siva. One dark night when Siva and Paravathi were journeying through the sky they saw a man perched on the branch of a tree, about to fall on the ground through sheer exhaustion of limbs. Parvathi pleaded on his behalf and wanted that Siva should save him; and Siva preferred that she should save him instead. Meanwhile, the fall became imminent and they decided that if while falling the man shouted "Amma", Parvathi should hasten to arrest his fall, and if he shouted, "Appa", Siva should help and see that no bones are broken. The man fell, but he shouted neither Amma or Appa but Ayyo! And so he had to be left severely alone!

THE FAITH OF THE DISCIPLE

In South India, in the Tamil country, there was a certain Adigal or Dasa, in a village, Thangalur by name. He had heard of the spiritual grandeur of Saint Appar and developed great admiration for him. So he built rest-houses in his name; named his children after him so that they might grow up in the halo of his glory; he donated lands and houses, all in the name of the Saint he had not seen. See how faith preceded experience here. There are others who require experience before they fix their faith. The first path is more thrilling and lasting.

Well, one day by chance Appar himself walked into Thangalur for he had missed his way and had to deviate. He noticed everywhere in the town Appar Rest-houses and Appar Charities, and wondered how his name had preceded him. Then Adigal ran forward to His Guru and took him home and prepared a grand feast for him. When his eldest son went to his garden to cut a few plantain leaves for a dinner, a snake bit him and he died on the spot. Adigal, however, was not affected in the least; he covered up the corpse, heaping dry leaves upon it and proceeded with the formalities of hospitality for the long- sought Guru. The Guru, however, insisted on all the children of Adigal sitting around him during the meal, and he ordered the father, "Go, call every one here." Adigal did as he was commanded. He called and the dead son rose. He too came and sat for dinner with the rest. When he knew what had happened, Appar said, "Your Bhakthi is greater than my Sakthi."

THE BROOM

There was an old man lying on his deathbed. He belonged to the Kannada country. While in his last moments he could only blabber some word, which his children could not understand; they called in a doctor and asked him to give oxygen or something so that the words might become clear; they surmised that he was announcing to them where exactly he had hidden the money he had earned. So, they did everything to get the words correctly. They could distinguish only one sound, Ka! So they asked whether he meant kanaka (gold), karu (calf), Kanaja (granary), kasabarke (broom)...! When the broom was shown, his head nodded and died. So, he had to take birth later as a broom! That was his last thought!

LAME EXCUSES

Once, Krishna and His comrades stole into a house and brought down the vessel of curds, when the mistress of the house came in. "Why did you come in?" She asked. "My mother had a stick in her hand; so, I ran in here out of fear," Krishna replied. "Who are these boys?" She asked. "I brought them to bear witness to what I say" replied Krishna. "Why have you placed that vessel between your legs?", she asked in feigned anger. "So that these fellows may not get hold of the butter", was the answer! "Why do you go from house to house and eat the butter from their stores?" Asked Yasoda. "I like only things I select and choose; I do not like to be fed", replied the Boy Krishna. Krishna could not be confined to one routine. He is Sarvavyapi; He is Bhaktha Vathsala.

THE DONKEY DIED

You must take every step in Sadhana or is Samsara, only after deep deliberation and satisfying yourself that it will be for your good. Otherwise, it will be like the story of the weeping city. One day, a close female attendant of the Queen came to the Palace weeping in great sorrow, and so the Queen began to shed tears. Seeing the Queen in tears, the entire zenana wept and the weeping spread to the male attendants also. The King, finding the queen inconsolably sad, also wept profusely in sympathy, and the sight made the entire city weep loud and nonstop. At last, one sensible fellow set in motion an inquiry, which passed through person after person until the queen herself was accosted. She said that her attendant was in sore grief; and when she, a washerwoman by caste, was interrogated, she confessed that it was all due to the sudden demise of her favourite ass! When this news spread the weeping ceased and there was widespread laughter and shame. Reason out, discriminate; do not rush to conclusions or be led away by mere hearsay.

THE RABBIT RAN

Wherever you go, you meet only Me. I am present everywhere. Have you heard the story of the Rabbit that had borrowed from Mother Earth four naye paise? She thought that if she moved into a new region she would be free from the obligation. So, one day she ran as fast as her legs could carry her and went far far away from the place where the amount was originally received. At last, she sat down in great relief and said to herself, "Now, no one will ask me to repay". What was her surprise when from the ground underneath she heard a voice: "Mother Earth is right under your feet, here. You cannot escape from me, however far you run".

So too, you cannot run away from Me. I will demand good conduct, good habits, good thoughts, good company, wherever you go, seeking for refuge.

FEAR KILLS

A Sanyasi once met the Cholera Goddess on the road, returning from a village where she had thinned the population. He asked her how many she had taken into her lap; she replied, "Only ten". But really speaking, the casualties were a hundred. She explained, "I killed only ten; the rest died out of fear!" Man is Atmaswarupa, that is, Abhayaswarupa. If he knows his real nature, he will give no room for weakness, cowardice.

SEND THEM TO GOD

Really speaking, the best way to gain happiness is to choose God as the leader and guide. Then, He will guide and guard, from the heart itself. Emperor Sivaji once sent some persons from the Court to Samartha Ramdas, his preceptor, with a large quantity of provisions-grain, clothes, sweets and vessels. He asked them. "For whom have you brought these and why?" They replied, "For you. You have no one who can provide for you, and so, Sivaji Maharaj has sent all this." Ramdas laughed and said, "I have Providence Itself to provide for me; God alone has no one to provide for Him. Ask Sivaji to send these things to God!"

ONAM

This day is celebrated as the day when Emperor Bali was both humiliated and blessed by God, in the Form of Vamana, Sovereign of the Three Worlds. Bali called himself so, for, he had Bala or power, more than any one else. He was saturated with egoism. God came to him, while he was busy with a Yaga, in the form and guise of a Brahmin boy, and asked for a gift of just three foot- measures of land. Bali told him that he could ask for infinitely more riches and lands; but, the Boy insisted on that tiny gift only. The preceptor of Bali warned him about the identity and bonafides of the strange mendicant; he mentioned that he may be God Himself. This made Bali happier, for, if it was true, he was so mighty that even God came to his door as a mendicant. Such was the measure of his conceit.

But, when Vamana drew Himself up to cosmic proportions and measured the entire earth with one foot and the vast expanse of space with another foot, Bali was humbled; he offered his own head as the third foot-measure, and let himself be trodden into the nether-world. This day marks the day when the incarnation of Vamana happened, in order to teach this lesson that pride meets with doom. Once the ego was thus suppressed, Bali became cleansed and God blessed him with various boons. He assured him that He would ever be his guardian. He permitted him every year, on Onam Day, to come up into the world and see for himself his empire and receive therefrom the homage of his people. So, this is the Festival of Vamana's advent as well as Bali's Transformation.

MANY VOICES

When you examine your mind, you will find voices there, holding sway, not one but many counsellors, with their contrariness, causing confusion. For example, no sooner have you planned to come to Puttaparthi to take the Darsan of Swami, these counsellors start playing their game. One voice advises you to start only after ascertaining whether Swami is actually present there. Another voice suggests that you can put through a call to 'so-and- so' and discover whether Swami is at Bangalore or at Puttaparthi. A fourth lays before you alternative routes and means of transport, and causes a good deal of headache. This is the Sangam, around the Jangam, the Sangam (group) of voices that play around the spirit of Right, trying to distract it. Another voice might say, when the others have finished, "Well, my dear man! Consider from all points of view this desire of yours. You may go there, putting yourself to a lot of expense and bother: think of this possibility also--you may or may not get an `interview' with Swami." Another voice might intervene and say, "O! Considering all the wrongs done and all the faults committed, it is very doubtful, if Swami will grant you the `interview'." In the wake of this Voice another will begin its argument of assurance. It will comfort, saying, "No! Swami is the very embodiment of compassion. He will certainly pardon all errors." This principle that guides and guards you along the spiritual path is the Lingam that is in the centre of the Consciousness clustering round the inner and outer senses.

IMITATION

In the Bhagavatham, there is mention of a certain Poundraka, who sought to become a possible 'imitation' of Krishna. He added unto his name the name of Krishna, viz, Vasudeva. He announced himself as Poundraka Vasudeva. He got made an imitation Conch and an imitation Wheel (out of wood) and carried them about, in his two artificial extra hands. He discovered the style which Krishna adopted while wearing his yellow silken robe and he scrupulously followed the same. He skilfully imitated the gait and gestures of Krishna. Some fools gathered round him, mistaking him to be the Lord they were seeking. His insanity finally brought about his downfall and humiliation.

HIS REFUGE

God is the embodiment of compassion. He watches for a grain of goodness or humility so that He can reward it with tons of Grace. In a certain temple for Siva, the priest had a silver basin with a hole in its base for water to drip continuously. He filled it with water and hung it over the Lingam (the idol of Siva) so that the God who swallowed the poison which would have destroyed the Universe could be cooled and comforted! Even at night when the doors of the shrine were locked by the priest as he went home, the silver basin of water was in its position. So, a thief broke into the sacred apartment; his eyes were on the silver; he could not reach the rope that kept the basin in position; so, he climbed on the Lingam itself in order to take the costly booty down. Even as he was standing on the holy idol, Siva manifested Himself in all His glory before him, saying, "Son! I appreciate your surrender; you have cast on me your entire burden." The thief prayed that Siva may help him to secure the silver; there was no ladder or bench or any other article on which he could climb. So, the Lingam was his only refuge.

WHERE HE IS NOT

Once a Guru sent a pupil for further guidance to a mendicant in a Siva temple. When he reached the temple, he found a fellow reclining in the central shrine with both his legs resting on the sacred Lingam. The pupil was naturally enraged at the man's insolence; when he spoke angrily against the behaviour, the man said, "Please lift my legs and place them where the Lingam is not." When he did so, there was a Lingam under the feet in the new position. Wherever he deposited the man's legs, a Lingam rose to give them rest! That was the lesson the beggar taught him--God is everywhere; win the vision to see Him so.

SIVA

Consider the significance of the Form that Siva has assumed for human adoration: In his neck, He has the holocaust-producing poison, Halahala, that can destroy all life in a trice. On his head, He has the sacred Ganga River, whose waters can cure all ills, here and hereafter. On his forehead, He has the eye of Fire. On His Head, He has the cool comforting Moon. On His wrists, ankles, shoulders and neck, He wears deadly cobras, which live on life-giving breath of air. Siva lives in the burial ground and the burning ghat, the Rudrabhumi as it is called-the Land of Siva or Rudra. The place is no area of dread; it is auspicious area, for all have to end their lives there, at the close of this life or a few more lives. Siva is teaching you that death cannot be shunned or frightened away. It has to be gladly and bravely met.

Siva, again, is said to go about with a begging bowl. He teaches that renunciation, detachment, indifference to good fortune or bad, these are the paths to him. Siva is known as Mrutyunjaya, He who vanquishes death. And He is also the Kaamaari, the destroyer of Desire. These two names show that he who destroys Desire can conquer Death, for Desire breeds Activity, Activity breeds Consequence, Consequence breeds Bondage, Bondage results in Birth and Birth involves Death.

Iswara is also symbolised in the Linga Form, Linga is derived from the Sanskrit root, Li, means Leeyathe, '\merges'; it is the Form in which all forms merge. Siva is the God who blesses beings with the most desirable gift of meaning, in the Universe. That is the end, the death, which one should strive for, the end which Siva can vouchsafe. Realise the God in you first; then, if you involve yourself with the material world, no harm can come to you, for you will recognise the objective world as but the Body of God. But, if you try to involve yourself with the objective world first, then you can discover God as material only. Again, you can direct your spiritual efforts in either of two ways; endeavour to reach Him. Follow the commands of God, and He will be pleased to raise you up. Follow the path of inquiry and discover where He resides, and realise Him there. You can follow either means. But, reaching Him is the inescapable task of man.

Siva means: Graciousness; Auspiciousness; Mangalam. He is all Graciousness, Ever-Auspicious, Sarva-mangalam. That is the reason why the epithet, Sri, which indicates these qualities, is not added to the Name Siva, Sankara, Iswara etc. It is added to the Names of Avatars, for they have taken on perishable bodies for a specific purpose. They have to be distinguished from other humans, by the epithet. Siva is eternally gracious, auspicious, mangala, and so the epithet is superfluous. Siva is adored as the Teacher of Teachers, Dakshinamurti. The Form of Siva is itself a great lesson in Tolerance and Forbearance.

The Halahala poison is hidden by Him in His Throat; the beneficent Moon which all welcome, He has worn on His Head. This is a lesson for man to keep away from others all harmful tendencies and to use for their benefit all useful tendencies that he can command. If one uses his skills for his own advance, and his evil propensities for putting down others, he is only taking the road to ruin.

THE TRIAL

Thyagaraja was invited by the Maharaja of Thanjavur, Sarfoji Maharaj, the descendent of Sivaji, so that he may be loaded with precious gifts or Nidhi! But, the poet- singer-mystic-saint took it as a temptation trying to entice him into error. He asked the question: Is Nidhi more valuable as giver of joy; or, is Sannidhi (Divine Presence) more useful for the purpose? Of course, the answer was clear. Thyagaraja's brother who was counting on the treasure which the Maharaja will bestow on him grew wild with anger at his refusal to go to the Durbar. He pushed his brother out of doors, and did not allow him to re-enter! He threw the idols, which he was worshipping, through which he had realised Rama as the indweller of everyone, into the flooded river!

Tukaram was honoured by the gift of a gorgeous palanquin and caskets of jewels by Sivaji. But, Tukaram said, ``Ram! I will not take my hands from off Your Feet, for, I know you are waiting to escape from me, the moment I release the grasp to hold anything other than your Divine Feet" When Thyagaraja passed away, his wife kept his head on her lap, and when the saint was calling out `Rama!' `Rama!' in ecstatic agony three hot tear-drops fell from her eyes, on the face of the dying Thyagaraja. `O, I am the property of Rama! But you are still the property of Kama!" Thyagaraja exclaimed. Sublimate the love you have for the pleasures of the world, for the objects of the world, into love for God. Do not waste even a single second, in idle scandal or hollow praise. Bend your head before God, welcoming whatever be His will; then, you too can have the Lord as your guide and guard.

VICTORY IS SURE

The last sloka of the Gita says, ``Yathra Yogeswarah Krishna Yathra Partho Dhanurdharah, Thathra Sreer Vijayo Bhuthi Dhruva Neethir Mathir Mama", where there is Krishna the supreme Yogi and where also there is Arjuna bearing his bow, there victory for truth and justice is assured". This verse assured victory not only when the Mahabharatha Arjuna wields the bow in the presence of Krishna. Every one of you can be Arjuna and wield the bow and achieve victory. For the bow is but the symbol of courage and faith, of high resolve and undaunted action. And how can you become Arjunas? Arjuna means white, pure, unsullied, without blemish. As soon as you become that and hold the bow (the Upanishads declare that the Pranava or Om is the arrow and God is the target), Krishna is ready with His presence, for He is everywhere at every moment. There is no need to invite Him or instal Him. He will answer from your very heart.

GO SLOW

There was a middle-class household in a small town, where the wife was daily pleading with the husband to spend some little time in prayer and reverential worship of God; but, the husband refused to yield, for, as he said, he had no time to spare for such pastimes which are best taken during old age, when the process of earning and spending receives a natural setback and there will be ample leisure. The pious lady could not derive any consolation from this reply. She could only wait for some more auspicious opportunity when her advice would fall on receptive ears.

Meanwhile, the husband was affected by serious illness and he was bed-ridden for a few weeks. The doctors advised him to take some tablets thrice a day. The wife accepted the task of administering the tablets and kept them with her; however, she did not give him even one!

The husband was put out by her intransigence; he demanded the tablets, but she was firm in her resolve. She said, in reply to his question, ``Are you conspiring to kill me?", ``Wait, wait. Why hurry to take medicine so soon? Let the illness become more serious; why all this haste? Go slow, Go slow. There is enough time, as you said when I wanted you to pray and do Namasmaran". The husband realised that his stand was foolish; so, he mended his ways, and cured himself of both types of illness.

BANANA COMPETITION

Two young men studying in the same college challenged each other--who can eat faster than the other, a prescribed number of bananas. They decided upon impartial umpires and stood before the banana baskets.

One young man resolved that if he eats the skins first, the sweet soft fruit inside can be no problem later; the other youth decided that once the soft portions were eaten fast he would have enough time to chew the skins. But, after finishing the skins the first young man had no stomach to swallow the kernel; he was too full. The other man had to stop as soon as he had finished the soft insides, for he had no more space inside him for the skins. Both failed in the competition; but, what a difference they had in their experiences!

The one had a surfeit of bitter stuff; the other, a surfeit of sweet! People resolve to experience God and

Godly company only after going through most of life. They eat skins and have no appetite for the kernel. The first place must be accorded to God; then, joy and peace will be the lot.

THE TONGUE AND THE EYE

There was a monk once who as the first two steps in ascetic practice decided on two vows: (1) not to injure any living thing and (2) not to speak falsehood. While he was engaged in meditation under a tree in the thick jungle, invoking the aid of God to confirm him in these two vows, he saw a beautiful deer, running in terror from some hunters and taking refuge in a bower behind his hermitage. The hunters came to him seconds later. They asked him about the whereabouts of the deer. The poor monk was in a fix. If he told them that he saw it entering the bower they would catch it and kill it. That will go against his first vow. If he told them that he does not know its whereabouts, it would be against his second vow. He avoided breaking both his vows in a very clever way. He said, "The eye that sees cannot speak. The tongue that speaks cannot see. I cannot compel the eye to speak, nor the tongue to see". The hunters went away quietly and the deer was saved. The monk had not uttered falsehood.

PHYSICAL BEAUTY

A certain Maharaja had an only son, who grew strong and well-built. When he was about 22 years of age, the father talked to him of marriage. The Prince wanted the father to allow him to choose his bride among his subjects. The Maharaja gladly agreed. One day, while the Prince was going on horseback along a bridge, he saw a damsel proceeding to the river below for her bath, and immediately fell frantically in love with that embodiment of beauty. She was the daughter of a Vaisya, a rich merchant of the City. The girl was highly religious, well-versed in all the holy scriptures and very much averse to worldly entanglements like marriage. When the courtiers from the palace sought out the Vaisya and asked him to consent to the marriage of his daughter with the Prince, they were surprised to find that the father was reluctant to agree. He considered that being a Vaisya, he should have only a Vaisya son-in-law. The daughter complicated affairs by saying that she would not marry at all. The palace threatened dire punishment for both father and daughter.

At last, the daughter hit upon a plan to escape punishment. She told her father to tell the Palace officers that she would like to meet the Prince face to face, eight days later and if the Prince still wanted to marry her, she was willing to do so. Then, she swallowed strong purgatives every day and collected the excreta each day in a separate vessel. On the eighth day, she was taken in a royal palanquin to see the Prince. She took with her the eight vessels well covered up and insisted that they too be placed in the Audience Hall, where she was to meet the Prince. None knew what they contained. The Prince was shocked to find before him a living skeleton of a girl, ghastly, with hollow cheeks and sunken eyes. He asked her, ``where is all that beauty gone?". She pointed to the eight vessels of excreta. The Prince, it need not be said, declined the marriage and the girl was happy she had taught him a lesson on the evanescence of physical charm.

WHO IS TO DIE?

Once in Puttaparthi, in a village play, the role of Vali was assigned to a rich man's son and that of Sugriva to a poor man's son. Then Vali protested that he would not die in the fight with the poor man's son and insisted that Rama should befriend him and kill Sugriva instead! The story cannot be changed to suit your whims. When the play says that Vali should die and when he has been given that role, he should die correctly just as He has decided.

THE FROG

While Rama, Sita and Lakshmana were roving among the hills and dales of Dandakaranya, one day Rama moved towards the bank of a clear blue lake. While stepping down the bank, Rama put his foot on a little frog, which suffered great pain but remained mute. Rama felt pity at the poor creature's plight and asked the frog, why it did not cry out in protest. The Frog replied, "Whenever I get into trouble or have fear from foes, I cry out, 'Rama! Rama!' but, when Rama himself is causing me pain, whom am I to appeal to?"

THE COW SHE WANTED

A woman visited the village fair to purchase a cow. She wandered along the long lines of cattle, brought for sale. She could not get the cow she sought. For she wanted a cow that was hornless, tame; she must have a female calf; she must eat very little grass; she must yield a good quantity of milk; she must give a sizeable quantity of dung, black-green in colour, so that she can use it for flooring her hut; she must be of the holy Kapila (brown, tawny or reddish) colour. No wonder she had to return disappointed.

NOT COPPER

Once a poet approached Bhoja for help and when the Emperor held before him a purse, he refused to accept it, because he said, "You must give me something which you have earned by the sweat of your brow, not something which you have appropriated from the earning of others' toil". The Emperor appreciated the argument; he asked him to call on him the next day. When the poet presented himself the next morning as directed, Bhoja gave him 16 copper coins which he had earned from a smithy, handling the hammer to beat the red hot iron. The poet held out his hand for it; the coins were given; but, what a wonder, they were gold coins, not copper. The toil of the king had made them pure gold. One must give only what one has legitimately earned. Then the dehi gives without deha consciousness.

LAND HUNGER

Some one had a hundred acres in the south; but he had an itching for more, at least a 1000. So he went in all directions seeking regions where he could get vast areas of uncultivated but cultivable land. At last, he came to a Himalayan kingdom and the King gladly offered to give him all the land he hungered for; the only limit he placed was his endurance. He said the man should start walking without tarrying; he should return to the starting point before the sun sets; all the land enclosed by his route, traced by his steps from start to finish, would be his. That was the generous offer the King made. The greedy migrant waited anxiously for the first rays of the rising sun and he started off on the circumference of a very wide circle, running in fact, until evening fell; he was so exhausted when he neared the starting point that within three yards of the starting spot, he dropped dead! His heart stopped beating. He had overworked it in his mad race to appropriate as many acres as he possibly could, before sunset.

HE WON

Honour your parents so that your children learn to honour you. There is a fine story mentioned in the Puranas about this. The Divine Parents, Siva and Parvathi, once laid down a test for their two sons Ganapathi and Subramanya. They were to go round the whole world and return to them; he who does it quicker will win the prize. Subramanya started quick and fast, and was pacing through highlands and lowlands, but Ganapathi walked quickly round the parents and claimed the prize. He said, the Parents are all the world and the statement was accepted as correct. Ganapathi was installed as the Deity supervising the acquisition of knowledge and as the Deity who shall save all aspirants from obstacles on their path. The moral of this story is that parents have to be cared for and obeyed. That is the real Pitryajna.

UNDER HIS OWN PILLOW

A rich merchant once went to a holy place, to attend the temple festival. A thief too followed him, in order to knock off his purse; but, he posed as a companion proceeding to the same place, for the same festival. They stayed in a Dharmasala for the night. When everyone had gone into deep sleep, the thief who kept awoke until then, rose and searched everywhere for the merchant's bag. He could not lay hands on it in spite of restless search. When day broke he told the merchant in a friendly manner, "There are thieves in this place; I hope you are taking good care of your bag, which holds all your money". The merchant replied, "O, Yes. Last night, I kept it right under your pillow. See, how safe it is". So saying, he took it from underneath the thief's pillow! God is like that merchant; he has placed the bag holding Atmasakthi, Atmajnan, and unalloyed happiness in the head of man. But, man is ignorant of this; he seeks to find it outside him.

MAGIC

When Krishna appeared at one time on one side, on the other side at another time, all around him sometimes, Kamsa scorned Krishna and said, ``You fellow! Krishna! Put a stop to your magic tricks!" He did not stop with that. He boasted ``Face to face with the might of my shoulders, the might of your magic, how much is it? Only a tiny drop!" When the same Krishna, a seven-year youngster vaulted over him and felled him to the ground and sitting on his chest, squeezed his neck in a mortal hold, Kamsa wailed piteously, ``O! Oh! I am dying! "Then, Krishna retorted, ``Uncle! This is magic! Magic, only magic!"

ABOUT TURN

God told a certain Sanyasin, ``Do not worry! I am always behind you." One day, the Sanyasin wanted to test whether God spoke the Truth. So, acting out of doubt, he quickly turned his head and did not see God. He asked God why He wasn't there; and God said, ``As you turned your head, I moved around to the back of your head! Naturally, you were unable to see me!" God is Truth, Truth is His Nature. Truth is His sign, His breath.

GRATITUDE

An ant was caught on a dry leaf that was being carried down a flooded river and it called out from its tiny heart to God for succour. God prompted a kite that was flying over the river to dive and rise up, with the leaf in its beak; for He made the bird mistake it for a fish or frog! The bird was sorely disappointed, but, the ant was delighted to land on hard ground! God came as a kite and rescued me, it felt. I must be grateful to the bird, to all birds, it resolved. One day, while on its morning round, it saw a hunter aim an arrow at a bird; remembering how its own life was saved by a bird, it bit the heel of the hunter, when he was about to release the mortal shaft; the aim failed; the bird flew off, and was saved. The ant had paid its debt.

THE TITLE AT LAST

Viswamithra was upset, that, despite years of asceticism, his great rival, Vasishta addressed him only as Rajarshi, and not by the coveted appellation, Brahmarshi; so, he crouched stealthily behind the seat of Vashista one moonlit night when he was teaching a group of disciples, determined to kill him with the sharp sword he had taken with him. He sat unseen amidst the bushes for a moment to listen to what Vashista was telling them. What was his surprise when he heard Vasishta describing the charming moonlight and comparing it to the heart of Viswamitra, cool, bright, curative, heavenly, universal, all-pleasing! The sword fell from his fell grasp. He ran forward and prostrating at the feet of his rival, he held the feet. Vasishta recognised Viswamitra and accosting him, ``O Brahmarishi, rise up", he lifted him on to his own seat. Vasishta explained that he could not be styled Brahmarshi, so long as the ego persisted in him. When the swelling of the head disappeared and he fell at the feet of his rival, he became entitled for the honour he no longer coveted, and so deserved.

FANTASY

A street-hawker had on his head a basket full of empty bottles, as he walked along to the bazaar. He hoped to sell the lot at a profit of ten rupees and, in ten days, he calculated his earnings would have accumulated to a hundred rupees; with that capital, he planned to switch on to more-profitable deals, so that he imagined he could make a pile of a lakh of rupees in a few months and build a bungalow with a lovely garden tended by a regiment of servants, beaming all round the house. There he saw himself on a sofa in the greenery playing with his grandchildren. He was engrossed in that charming scene; suddenly he saw among his grandchildren, the child of one of the servants; he got angry at this unwanted intrusion. Believing his fantasy to be a reality, he suddenly grabbed the child and gave it a swift hefty push--only to find that the basket of bottles had fallen on the road and all hopes of even the ten rupees lost! That was the end of a dream built on the slender basis of greed.

MUTUAL HELP

A man sees while going along a road a ripe fruit, on a tree by the side. The mind craves for the fruit, but, that by itself cannot fulfil that craving. The feet take him near the tree. But, that does not bring about the consummation. The trunk stoops, the hand picks up a stone, the shoulders throw the stone at the fruit, and the fruit falls on the ground. But, that does not end the story. The fruit has to be picked up by the fingers, transferred into the mouth, the teeth have to bite into it, and masticate it well, and the tongue has to take charge in order to make it reach the stomach. The eating part of the task is thus over.

But, that does not end the story of the craving for the fruit. Since so many instruments co-operated in the fulfilment, gratitude has to be rendered to each of them. So, the stomach sends strength and satisfaction to every limb that shared in the adventure of securing the fruit and eating it--the eye, the feet, the hands, the fingers, the shoulder, the tongue, the teeth, the gullet. No one of them is neglected or discriminated against.

THE VOMIT

A person saw in the hollow of his hands the shadow of a lizard as he was doing his ceremonial rite in the river with water; and, he swallowed the sacred water, without seeing whether it was just a shadow or the real thing. Later, he was bothered by the fear that he had swallowed the poisonous thing. And he developed all the symptoms of lizard poisoning, until a wise man came by and procuring a lizard, made it wriggle in the vomit that was induced in the unfortunate victim. When the poor man saw the lizard that presumably came out of his stomach, he was happy and he recovered. Man too suffers from a similar delusion, imagining himself to be afflicted by something that is purely a creation of his own ignorance.

COME TOMORROW

While life lasts, use every moment for the Sadhana which will lead you Godwards. One day a poor Brahmin arrived at the court of Dharmaraja, the eldest of the Pandavas, pleading for where with all for the celebration of his daughter's marriage. Dharmaraja promised to give him all that he needed, but, he asked him to come the next day. At this, Bhima was so elated that he ordered the event to be celebrated with beating of drums and hoisting of flags all over the kindom. When the King inquired the reason for this sudden spurt of joy, Bhima replied, “You have now announced that you will live one more day; is that not enough cause for joy, when every one else is uncertain of even the next moment?"

THE GIFTS

This life has been given to you to search and search for God. You have been given eyes and vision to help you to see the Supreme One, the Omnipotent Divinity. The legs are given to enable you to visit the Temple of God. The hands have been given to you to perform Puja with flowers to the Lord. You have been provided with intelligence so that you may realise that all that you see around is a very temporary and transient phenomenon. You have been given a mouth to sing the Glory of the Lord. Ears have been given to you to listen to songs relating to the Glory of a God. You have been given a human body for doing Good to other human beings. You should put into practice the principles and codes of conduct and surrender your Ego at the Lotus Feet of God residing in the heart.

A BRICK FOR HIS GOD

Pundaleek, a great devotee of Panduranga, was one day massaging the feet of his mother. Then, his Panduranga, the Form of God he had installed in his heart and shrine, came in all his splendour and stood before him ! What a temptation to give up the service of the mother and rush towards the Feet of his God ! But Pundaleeka said-"Please wait a few moments. I shall finish this service and then, offer homage to You." He threw a brick for Panduranga to stand upon, for it is the first step in hospitality, to offer a seat for the guest.

Pundaleeka's Guru, Kabir, told him that one does service to the mother so that grace of God can be won; but even then, he did not give up the service in the middle. Such was the steadfastness and his faith.

THE MOST LAUDABLE CHOICE

The Yaksha on the tree had stopped the five Pandava brothers from drinking at the lake below, for, it put questions to each of them and when they could not answer to its satisfaction, they died- four of them ! It was Dharmaraja, the eldest, who came last. He was able to answer the questions correctly. So, the Yaksha said, "well, You can now revive and take ONE of the four brothers who are lying here dead." Dharmaraja had the hardest of problems, but, he did not take long to select. He did not revive either Bheema or Arjuna, though they were for him as his two hands. He selected Nakula. The Yaksha asked him why he had chosen him. He said, "I, Bhima and Arjuna are the sons of Kunti and Nakul and Sahadeva are the sons of my step-mother, Madri. My mother has me alive ; so I wished my step-mother too to have a son alive. So I chose one of her sons." What a noble heart was his ! At this Yaksha was so pleased that he revived all the four.

THE DHOBI REPLIES

Once a big argument arose between a Dualist and a Monist (a Dwaithin and an Adwaithin). The Monist said that jiva is not really Jiva, but is, genuinely Deva; that the Individual is God; that all is God. The Dualist would not agree, even though many quotations were given by Monist from Vedas etc., to prove the point. The Dualist accosted a dhobi who was passing along the road and asked him," Hello ! Tell us who you are? Are you God?" He got frightened at the suggestion; he said; "No, I am only I." Then the Dualist said, " Did you hear? Even the man in the street knows that he is not God and that he is only a Jivi". The Adwaithin replied, "No. He said that I am 'I'. Every one from the Emperor down to the man in the street says, I am 'I'. Now, that 'I' is the reflection of God in the individualised body"

WHICH ONE TO HOLD?

A pilgrim going to a forest shrine was overtaken by night and, unable to see his way, he slipped into a well. Luckily, while falling he chanced to hold the root of a tree hanging loose by the side of the well. When morning dawned, a Sadhu came to the neighbourhood of the well and sang few songs on God. The pilgrim shouted to him and when he saw the plight of the poor fellow, the Sadhu let down a length of sturdy rope, so that he could pull him up and save him. The pilgrim was now in two minds--whether to hold on to the root or hold the rope? Of course it was silly; one should hold on to the root only until the rope is available. So too, when God is realised, all Karma must drop off.

INTIMATIONS OF MORTALITY

One merchant who was very much afraid of death worshipped the God of Death, Yama, for many years and offered elaborate Puja to Him. Yama was pleased at the special attention and adoration shown by him and promised that he will not pounce upon him all of a sudden, but will give him advance intimation, so that he can put his affairs in good trim before leaving the world. When at last, his end came and he was about to die, he got wild with Yama and in his anger, he charged Yama with falsehood, ingratitude and cheating. He said that he was not given any advance intimation at all. But, Yama said, "Why? I had sent you not one but four intimations, well in advance of this consummation." The merchant said that he had not received any of them. But, Yama said, "Your hair turned grey. That was the first intimation. But, you dyed it and forgot its lesson. I made you bald, but, you wore a wig and slighted the notice I gave. Then, I had all your teeth fall off; you wore a denture and pretended I was far away. The fourth intimation I sent was folds all over your skin. You did not pay heed to that warning, too". Indeed Yama had kept His word.

STOP! STOP! TURN BACK!

When Rama, Sita and Lakshmana were riding off to the Forest in the chariot, in obedience to the plighted word of Dasaratha, Dasaratha came in another chariot, behind them and shouted, in great agony at their departure, "Stop! Stop! Turn back!". But, Rama told the charioteer, Sumanthra, the Minister attached to the Court of Dasaratha, "Do not stop. Go faster". Sumanthra pleaded that he was an officer who must obey the Emperor and that he may be punished for disobedience. Rama told him, "Tell him that you did not hear his orders". "But that would be a lie", said Sumanthra. "No. He had asked you to take us out of Ayodhya in this chariot, as the Emperor. Now, he is asking you to stop, not as Emperor, but as a grief-stricken father. You must listen to the command of the Emperor, of course. You have no right or duty to listen to agony-stricken fathers wishing to have a look at their sons." Rama taught Sumanthra the true Dharma in this manner. A grief-stricken man cannot have a proper appraisal of what is right and wrong.

THE MOTHER CAT

The Mother Cat, it is said, carries its newly born kittens, still with unopened eyes, from house to house, depositing them in seven different homes. By the time the seventh house is reached, the kittens open their eyes and can see well and clearly. Man changes home every birth. But, his eyes do not open to the truth of God, even after his changing home (lives) many and many a time.

THE GERUA CLOTH

One day, when Swami Vivekananda was moving about in the City of Calcutta, an aristocratically dressed person accosted him and asked, "Why do you wear this gerua robe? Perhaps, you want to advertise that you have given up the world and renounced all desires. This exhibition is a sign of ego". Swami Vivekananda laughed and said, "My dear friend! I have no such idea. I wear it because seeing that I am a sanyasin, with no money, no beggar would approach me and bother me. I can walk about without being pestered. I have spiritual treasures with me, but, no cash. When people come asking for them, I give".

HE ASKED FOR IT

When Babhruvahana, the son of Arjuna, took hold of the horse that was to be sacrificed ceremoniously at the Aswamedha to be celebrated by the Pandavas, he did not know that it was his father who had come to retrieve the horse from captivity. When he knew that Arjuna had come, he moved forward and fell at his feet. When his mother heard about his quiet submission, she got enraged at his cowardice. "Being a Kshatriya, how could you yield the horse you have laid hands on, without a fight? Let him, even if it be your father, win it on the battlefield", she said. So, the battle took place between father and son and, believe it or not, Arjuna fell dead when the arrows of Babhruvahana struck him on the chest.

The son lamented his fate and wept aloud at the calamity that he had inflicted on his mother and on the world. Just then, Ulupi, a Naga Princess from the Nether world, appeared there and comforted Babhruvahana and the rest. She narrated the true story of the event, which showed that Arjuna had himself prayed for such an end. During Kurukshetra battle, Arjuna had let loose the Brahmastra, the most mortal of all lethal weapons, at Bhishma and that had led to his ultimate death. But, instead of joy at the death of the mighty general of the Kaurava forces, Arjuna was overwhelmed by remorse. Bhishma had brought up the Pandava brothers lovingly and with care after the death, while they were yet children, of their father, Pandu. He was the Pithamaha or Grandfather, of all of them. Now that he had himself caused his death, Arjuna cursed himself for having done so. He wished, "Let me be killed by my own son, as compensation for this ungrateful act of mine". Ulupi described this background story and soon, revived Arjuna back to life, with the mysterious powers she had accumulated in the Nether world. Every incident that looks absurd or wonderful, inexplicable or impossible, that is mentioned in the Puranas has a deeper meaning and significance.

SWEETER THAN TANSEN

Akbar was happy whenever Tansen, his court musician, sang. Tansen was the greatest musician of his day. When he sang the raag Meghamala, clouds thickened in the sky; when he sang the raag Varuna, showers of rain fell. When he sang the Naagaswara, snakes gathered. Akbar was very proud that he had, in his Durbar, a musician of such eminence.

But one day, while he was engaged in prayer, he heard the distant music of Haridasa, a wandering minstrel, a beggar singing to the tune of a single-stringed instrument he held in his hand, and Akbar was thrilled, enchanted, deeply moved.

He asked Tansen why that song appealed to him, more than all the songs Tansen sang in the Durbar. Tansen replied, "Lord! I sing, looking at your face to see any sign of appreciation, in the hope that you will give me a few gems or some acres of land. He sings looking at the face of God, with no greed for material wealth or ambition for earthly goods. That is the difference".

THE CUP AND THE NEEDLE

Thiruvalluvar, the renowned Tamil Saint, who has written the immortal work called `Kural', used to keep by his side, when he sat for meals, a needle and a small cup filled with water. Once, his host asked him why he insisted on having these two placed by the side of the plate. He said, "Food should not be wasted. Even a grain is precious. Sometimes, stray grains of cooked rice or stray pieces of cooked vegetables fall off the plate or away from it, while I eat; then, I lift them off the floor, with the help of this needle and stir them in the water to clean them, and eat them." What a great lesson this is, for those who waste more than they consume!

TIT FOR TAT

There was a Court Poet in the Durbar of the Emperor of Vijayanagar, called Lingapurana Sooranna, since he was an expert in expounding the text Lingapurana. He was envious of Tenali Ramakrishna, another Court Poet who had far greater talents. One day, Sooranna was at home composing a lampoon against Tenali Ramakrishna, in quite a ribald style. He was halfway through, when he received a call from the Emperor. So, he left the manuscript on his table and hurried to the Palace. Then, Mother Kali, the Goddess who was the patron deity of Ramakrishna, appeared before him and asked him to go to Sooranna's house and himself finish the lampoon. He did so and when Sooranna returned home, he was dismayed to find that the lampoon was an attack on himself, on his low and vulgar envy towards others far greater in poetic talent. Divinity cannot tolerate the besmirching of true devotees by envious and malignant minds.

THE SON-IN-LAW

A conceited, greedy son-in-law went to his mother-in-law's house. She was very poor, managing the household with great difficulty. However, she rendered him hospitality far beyond her means, borrowing from all and sundry. But, the fellow stayed on, and showed no intention to depart. The number and taste of the dishes at lunch and dinner became less and less; still, he did not plan to leave. She then tried some Vedantic philosophy. She sermonised on the evanescence of physical joys, the triviality of sense satisfaction etc. The fellow reacted in another way, the opposite way. He said, "Dear mother-in-law! I hold another view; you cannot change it by Vedanta. I know even the Gods declare by their action that the mother-in-law's home is more secure and more desirable than one's own. Siva lives in the Himalayas, and His Consort is the daughter of the Himalayas. Vishnu is ever on the Ocean of Milk, where Lakshmi was born." The mother-in-law had at last to resort to desperate measures. She quietly locked the fellow out and escaped to another village.

THE EYES I WANT

Surdas was a blind mystic, singer and poet. Lord Krishna once appeared and asked him, in His infinite mercy, if he wanted eyes, so that he could see the world. Surdas replied, "Though people have the kind of eyes you are offering to give me, they are befogged with ignorance and are not able to recognise You in all forms and in all beings. Though people have ears, they cannot hear the melody of your flute. I want eyes that can always see Your beauty everywhere; ears that can hear Your flute, from every corner of the world".

RAVANA AS RAMA

Ravana tried all methods to persuade Sita to yield, enter his Zenena and become his consort. He threatened her with instant death; he enticed her with gifts and promise of more. He tried soft words and cruel torture. At last, he hit upon a brilliant idea. He assumed the form of Rama and thought that she would be misled by that impersonation. But, as soon as he assumed that form, all evil thoughts fled from him and only ideals of righteousness held away. So, he had to give up that trick as useless.

LOVE GOD OR BE LOVED

Abou Ben Adhem saw a brilliance in his room when he returned home. He found an angel sitting at the table and recording something in a register. He ventured to ask her very politely what she was so assiduously writing down. She said that she was recording the names of those who loved God. Abou was a kind soul who helped the poor, shared his food and shelter with the hungry and the homeless; he was ever engaged in wiping tears off the facing of the sad. He had no particular loyalty to any God. He loved persons following all religions, provided they were good and kind. He cared only for the broad heart and the controlled mind. The Angel said, "No. Your name is not here."

Next day, Abou's home was again lit with the same brilliance, in the centre of which was found the same recording Angel. She had another Register now. Abou asked her what she was recording in that Register. She said, "I am writing down the names of those who are loved by God." Hesitatingly and with great temerity, Abou asked her whether his name was in that Register. The angel put her finger on the very first entry and said, "See ! Your name is the very first. Love your fellowmen; that is the best method to earn the Grace of God."

THE GASH ON THE BACK

There lived on the banks of the sacred Ganga a poor Brahmin, who was an ardent student of the Bhagavadgitha. He read it every day; he worshipped the Book and he tried to live according to its teachings. But, his faith was sorely tried, for he was immersed in distressing poverty. His bowl was seldom filled; he and his wife were on half ration all the time.

One day, while overcome by grief at his misery, his eye fell on the 22nd sloka of the 9th Chapter, where the Lord assures that He will bear the burden of all who take refuge in Him. He felt that in his case, the assurance was hoax and so, he took his pen and dipping it in red ink, he struck out the exasperating line ! Somewhat relieved of anger, he rose and went out with his bowl.

Before long, two boys, brothers by appearance, the younger of darker hue, came to his door, with a bag of rice and a basin of sundry other provisions. The wife was surprised, because they insisted all of it was for her and her husband ! She found a bleeding gash on the back of the younger boy, and when she asked him, who had inflicted the cruel wound, the reply was, "Your husband!" How could he lose temper so much as to stab such a charming child, she wondered. But, the brothers disappeared in a flash.

The husband knew nothing about the bleeding boy. He pleaded innocence. He wondered who could have sent them help. His head was in a whirl. As always, he turned to the Githa for consolation. The book opened on the 9th Chapter, sloka 22. Ah! His eye fell on the angry gash he had drawn on that page, across that line.

That pen had gashed Sri Krishan's back ! His want of faith had "wounded" Him. So He ran about like mad, to discover the Boy and fall at his feet, crying for mercy. But, he could not be found.

So, have faith in the Assurance of the Lord; when He says "Why fear, I am here". He means it; when he says, "I look to you when you look to Me", He means it.

FATHER LEAPS TO SAVE THE SON

You may ask, why should the Lord Himself incarnate? Why can He not set about the task of restoring Dharma through the many minor gods He has at His command? This question was posed before the courtiers by Akbar himself, for, he laughed at the Hindu idea of the Formless adopting Form, and descending into the world, as an Avathar to save Dharma. Tansen asked for a week's time to furnish the answer and got it granted by His Imperial Majesty. A few days later, when he was in the pleasure boat of the Emperor sailing across the lake with his family, Tansen cleverly threw overboard a doll made to look like the emperor's little son, crying at the same time, "O, the Prince has fallen into the water!" Hearing this, the Emperor jumped into the lake to rescue his son!

Tansen then disclosed that it was only a doll and that the son was safe. He allayed the anger of Akbar by explaining that he had perforce to enact this drama, in order to demonstrate the truth of the Hindu belief that God takes human form Himself, to save Dharma, without commissioning some other entity to carry out that task. Dharma is as the son, God loves it so dearly. Akbar could have ordered one among the many personnel he had on board, to jump in and rescue his son; but, his affection was so great and the urgency so acute that the Emperor himself plunged into the lake, to pull out the "son". The Decline in Dharma is so acute a tragedy the intensity of affection that the Lord has for good men is so great, that He Himself comes.

POSITION OF VANTAGE

You know that the Garuda bird feeds on snakes. Well, once Garuda went to Kailasa Mount to pay respects to Siva, who wears snakes on His head, arms, wrists, neck, waist and ankles. When the snakes saw Garuda, they were unafraid; they even dared put out their forked tongues at Garuda and challenged to come near them. That was the extent of the courage lent to them by the place where they had established themselves. So, establish yourselves in the Atma; no worry or grief or pride can harm you then.

ALEXANDER AND THE SAGE

Alexander, during his campaigns in the Punjab, was anxious to see a celebrated sage; he went to the cave where the sage was, and expected that he would be received most thankfully and with demonstrations of welcome. But, the sage simply asked him to move aside and go. He was not interested in the famous world-shaker, the Greek conqueror. Alexander was very angry; he threatened to kill the sage and drew his sword. But, the sage said calmly, with a laugh "I do not die, I am the Atma; I cannot die". That put some sense in Alexander and he put his sword back into the scabbard.

BOATMAN'S PRIDE

A man engaged a boat to take him across the flooded Godavari. When the journey over the river started, he began a lively conversation with the boatmen. He asked him whether he had any schooling and when the reply came that he had none, he said sadly, "Alas! A quarter of your life has gone to waste. It is as if you have drowned those years in the Godavari". He asked him whether he could tell him the time from his watch; the boatman confessed he did not have a watch nor cared to have one. The Pundit deplored and said, "Half your life has gone into the Godavari". His next question was about newspapers; did the boatman read any? What was his favourite paper? The boatman replied that he did not read any nor did he care to know the news. He had enough to worry about already. The Pundit declared forthright that three quarters of the boatman's life had been wasted. Just then the sky darkened with storm clouds and there was an imminent threat of rain. The boatman turned to the Pundit: It was his turn to put a question. He asked "Can you swim?" and when the frightened passenger confessed he could not, the boatman said, "In that case, your entire life is now going to merge in the Godavari". This is the case of the educated in India today. They do not have the training that will help them in distress, or in dire need, to win back their mental poise.

BEWARE

You must be aware of the danger of a fall, in time. Do not behave like the master of a house, who when his wife said, "I hear some noise; it is perhaps a thief", replied "I know; do not interrupt my sleep!" In a few minutes, she said, "He has entered the house", but the man said, "I know". Later she said, He is opening the box"; still, the man said "I know" and kept quiet. After sometime, she said, "He is running away" and the master said as formerly, "I know". He did not pay any attention to the warnings of the theft; so, too, you do not heed the warning, but move into the calamity, with eyes open.

NO PLACE TO DIE

There was a Sadhaka once who was initiated by a Yogi into some Manthram; he wanted to meditate on it undisturbed and he found his home too full of distraction. He fled to the forest and discovered a convenient tree, under which he could meditate. Before long, the birds roosting on its branches started to clamour aloud and they showered on his head their droppings. He was greatly incensed. "Have I no place where I can commune with God?" he cried. "Children at home, birds and bats in the jungle! I shall immolate myself, get born under better auspices and then start Sadhana afresh he decided. So, he collected a pile of fuel and making a pyre out of it, lit it and was about to ascend it, when he was interrupted by an old man who accosted him. He said, "By all means, carry out your decision; but, just now, the wind blows from here towards those huts where we live; so, please wait until the wind turns its direction, for, the smell of burning human flesh does not agree with us. Or, if you are in hot haste, you can shift to some other place and avoid being a nuisance to us poor folk". The Sadhaka felt he had no freedom even to die. So, he returned home, and decided to brave it all there itself. He understood that Karma has to be carried through in the objective world itself and there is no use trying to shake it off in a huff.

THE IDOL TURNED

When Kanakadas yearned to see the idol of Krishna, installed in the temple at Udipi, though he could not go into the sacred precincts, the Flag Post hid the view; so, he went round the shrine and tried to find a crevice in the wall, through which he could gain a glimpse of the Krishna he loved so much. He found a crevice; but, that gave him a glimpse of the back of the idol, not the resplendent face of the Lord. When he lamented his fate, the Idol turned round(!)-as can be seen even today--and gave him the coveted Darsan! That is the reward for the yearning.

INNER GANGA

There was a lady who attended a whole series of Bhagavatha discourses, and picked up a few cliches. She became too lazy to draw water and slept on till a late hour. When her husband reprimanded her, she quoted a sloka which said that one has in oneself all the holy rivers, Ganga, Yamuna, Saraswathi, as the Ida, Pingala and Sushumna nadis! The husband was astounded at her impudence and pseudo-spiritual pose. He contrived to feed her on highly salted stuff and he removed all the water pots and jugs from the house. When she suffered from acute thirst, and called out for water desperately, he quoted the same sloka and wanted her to draw from the Ganga, Yamuna and Saraswathi within her!

THE DONKEY'S THIRST

Adore the God that is resident in all beings, motivating them and prompting their every activity. Ekanath, the Maharashtra saint, had that vision. He was going on a pilgrimage to Rameswaram, in the extreme south of India, from Varanasi in the North, carrying the sacred Ganga in a pot, to be poured ceremoniously on the Ramalingeswara idol at the palace. His disciples were with him. On the way he saw a donkey dying of thirst, in great agony. Ekanath felt that the Ramalingeswara in the donkey was calling out for the holy Ganga that he was carrying on his shoulder; in spite of the protests of his followers, he poured the precious Ganga down the throat of the dying animal and saved it. His joy knew no bounds. God is the seed of all this manifested universe.

THE SEEING EYE

To be able to perceive good qualities, there is an example in Mahabharata. Krishna called Duryodhana with the intention of testing him. This took place before the war. Krishna told him that he wanted to do something important and that he was on the lookout for a good man with good attributes. He asked Duryodhana to look for such a man. He searched the world over for a few days and said that there was no person with really good attributes and if there was any one with good qualities, the best was himself and that he came nearest to the ideal. Then Krishna sent Duryodhana away and asked Dharmaraja to come. He told Dharmaraja to look for a man who is very bad and whose qualities are such that there can be no one else worse than him. Dharmaraja searched the world over and came back and told Krishna that he could not find anyone, it was himself. He said he fits the description which Krishna gave. For Duryodhana to say that he was the best man and for Dharmaraja to say that he was the worst man, the world is not responsible. The qualities in them and the way they look at themselves and at others are responsible. That is why we gave so much importance to the ability to perceive the good and distinguish it from the bad. No one can really determine what is bad. The only alternative is for one to have faith in God and improve his own qualities.

BEGGING FROM BEGGARS

A Fakir went to see Akbar and he was told that Akbar was at his prayers and so could not give audience for some time. He was asked to wait in the ante-room. But, he refused to wait; he said, "What can this beggar get from that beggar?" All are beggars at the gate of God. The hero is he who does not beg or cringe or flatter or fawn. He knows that the Lord knows best. If it is His Will He will grant food and raiment; if not, well, let His Will prevail.

THE FIVE-COW WOMAN

You judge a person by his conduct, his character as revealed in his actions. No other witness or proof is needed. There were two women, living opposite each other, in a Bazaar; one had five cows and the other had just one. The richer woman was wasteful in habits, very extravagant and careless. So, she used to borrow milk from the woman with one cow, and the latter was helping her, in spite of the fact that she had a large family. When she had thus borrowed about 50 seers of milk, the cow of the poorer women died, and she went to the other woman and wanted her to return the milk loaned, at the rate of a seer per day. At this, she got wild and deposed in court that she had never borrowed any milk.

"Why should I, owning five cows, go to this woman with one cow for the loan of milk?" she asked. The magistrate was a shrewd man who sympathised with the woman whose cow had died. He knew how to get at the truth. He gave each of them five "chembus" of water and asked them to wash their feet and come back to court. The five-cow-woman poured all the five chembu-full in one stream on her feet and came in with all the dirt intact. The one-cow-woman cleaned her feet by skilful use of one chembu-full only and she left the other four chembus untouched. The act of washing the feet revealed their character and the magistrate had no hesitation in convicting the culprit. The one-cow-woman must have saved and the five-cow-woman must have wasted and been in perpetual want.

THE COMMON TONGUE

There was a man from Puttaparthi who lived in a solitary hut on the banks of the Ganga some miles above Haridwar. He was engaged in severe Thapas and was greatly admired by other monks. One day, while bathing in the river, he overheard a party of pilgrims who had alighted from their bus at that site, talking among themselves in Telugu. His attachment to the mother-tongue dragged him thither; he asked them where they came from. They said Rayalaseema; he probed further; they were from Anantapur District; his ears ached for further details. They were from Penukonda Taluk, Puttaparthi itself, in fact. So, the monk was very happy; he asked them about his lands, his family, his friends and when he was told that a few of them had died, the poor fellow started weeping like a fool. All his years of Sadhana had come to naught. They broke down before the onslaught of language attachment. He was so bound to his mother tongue. What a pity!

Practise detachment from now on; practise it little by little, for a day will come sooner or later when you will have to give up all that you hold dear.

BRICKS OF GOLD

When Darmaraja decided in a fit of repentance to celebrate three Aswamedhas in a row, in order to win the Grace of God for the sin of slaughtering millions in the Kurukshetra battle, he had no money with him, nor could his vassal rulers help with finance! They too were impoverished by the war. And Krishna said, "Kings derive money only from the hard toil of their subjects. To spend on a Yaga done in expiation for the sins that threaten you the money squeezed out of their sweat is very wrong, it will be further sin."

So, Dharmaraja was in a fix. He pleaded with Krishna for helping him out. Then, Krishna told him "In bygone times, a ruler named Maruth performed a Yaga in a style that no ruler has approached so far. Gold bricks were given away as gifts to the priests, scholars and ritualists. Gold models of cows and houses and gold plates were given in thousands to the poor and the needy. When the recipients struggled along with the heavy load, they had to throw away many bricks and models, for they were too tired. They are available now, on both sides of the road they took. I know the place. Go, and collect them".

But, Dharmaraja hesitated. He said. "They belong to those to whom they were given. How can we use them without their permission?" Krishna replied, "They have willingly cast them away. They are not alive today. This took place long, long ago. They are under the earth. All treasure-troves belong to the ruler. You are the ruler. No one has the right to object". So, the gold was brought and the three Yagas were celebrated.

THE CAMERA

Our mind is like the lens of a camera. If you want to get the picture of the people on the right side, and you turn the camera to the left, how can you succeed? Our body is the camera, our mind is the lens, our heart is the photographic plate, our thought is the flash bulb, our buddhi or intelligence is the switch. If you want peace and happiness imprinted on your heart, turn the lens towards the activities and things that can give them, without any mixture of sorrow and misery.

GOD'S PLAN

When the Yadavas, the clansmen of Krishna, fought against each other a fratricidal battle and destroyed themselves completely, Dharmaraja asked Arjuna, "Could not Krishna stop it?" Arjuna said, "The fate of the Yadavas is the same as ours. We too Pandavas and Kauravas, brothers and Kinsmen, slaughtered each other. We had Krishna in our midst. He willed both battles. No one can cross His Will or act against his command".

THE OWNER OF THE KILL

Arjuna was lost in meditation on Siva, during his life as an ascetic in the Himalayan valley. Suddenly, a huge wild boar ran across the place where he was and evidently standing at bay, was grunting ferociously and snorting in terrible anger. Though during the penance, he should not hurt any living being, he hastily took up his bow and shot an arrow at the monster. Just at that moment, a Bhil of the forest, also armed with bow and arrow, appeared on the scene and claimed the boar as his kill. "Who are you, intruder, daring to shoot at my prey?", he shouted and he was in a defiant mood. Arjuna felt deeply insulted by the forest-dwelling tribesman. "The forest and its wild life are the property of all", he claimed. "Why did you kill the boar I was stalking?" asked the Bhil. From words they soon came to arrows. Arjuna noticed that his arrows fell off the Bhil, like blades of grass. He stood helpless and full of rage. He dealt a fierce blow with his bow on the head of the Bhil, but the bow it was that broke. He engaged the Bhil with his fists. They struggled long, dealing hammer blows on each other, but, it was Arjuna who flopped on the ground. The Bhil was not exhausted in the least, though Arjuna was gasping for breath, and bleeding. Then Arjuna realised that the Bhil was no ordinary mortal. He moulded a Linga of the Siva he was adoring and offered some flowers on it. And, he saw those flowers on the head of the Bhil and of his wife, who had joined him meanwhile. He was overcome with delight, for, he now knew they were Siva and His Consort, Parvati, come to test his fortitude and bless him.

THE CURSE THAT WAS WELCOMED

King Parikshith said, "I went into the forest a-hunting. Many wild animals were sighted but they scattered at our approach. The band of bowmen I had with me scattered in their pursuit. I found myself alone. I was far away from my retinue. I was overcome with hunger and thirst; the scorching heat exhausted me.

"At last, I discovered the hermitage of a sage. His name, I discover now, was Samika. I called out several times to draw the attention of those inside, so that I could get a little drinking water. No answer came; no one came out. So I myself went in. I saw a hermit sitting unconcerned, lost in what, for him, was meditation and what for me was utter disregard of my status and needs. I felt something soft under my feet. I found it was a dead cobra. My intelligence was poisoned. A foul thought came to me. I placed it round the neck of that sage, and chuckled within myself that it was some punishment for neglecting me. I came away to my City and palace.

But, the son of the sage saw his father with the dead cobra round his neck! He knew I had done it. So he cursed me, 'May the King die of snake-bite seven days from today.' Seven days! How kind of him! He could have cursed me to meet with death the very instant. He has given me seven days, to dwell on God and prepare myself to reality so that I can reach the Ultimate! What a great mercy! Few people get this week's notice when Death threatens".

UNOCCUPIED THRONES

When Bharatha, Satrughna and the Royal Queens, along with the huge civil and military retinue accompanying them, reached the Ashram of the great Sage Bharadwaja, he consoled them and assured them that Rama, Lakshmana and Sita were not very far off and that the moment they set their eyes on Rama, their grief would disappear.

Using his miraculous powers or Siddhis, Bharadwaja arranged hospitality for the Princes, the Queens, the Preceptors and Pundits, the Ministers and Generals, as well as the citizens and courtiers, each according to his status, in the most lavish style. Everything was produced mysteriously but plentifully, through his Will.

When the Reception Hall was ready, the Sage invited every one inside that marvel of beauty and grace. The Royal Preceptor was led to a high seat magnificently designed and covered with deerskin. The Queens were led into a special enclosure, cordoned off, as befits the Imperial zenana. Then the bright-faced disciples of the Sage brought in the two brothers into the Hall. The young ascetics stood respectfully on both sides waving yak-tail whisks and reciting Vedic hymns. The brothers, Bharatha and Satrughna, approached the Lion thrones set for them in the centre of the Hall and, as they came near them, they fell on the floor in reverential homage to their unseen occupants. Then, they took the whisks from the boys nearby and started waving them, in honour of the occupants of the Lion Thrones "Sita and Rama! The entire assembly was thrilled with joyous appreciation of their humility and wisdom.

LET THESE BE HERE ITSELF

The Superintendent of a District Jail called the prisoner to his Office and read out his discharge order. He said that he was free and had to get out of the Jail in half an hour. "While going, carry with you the mat and pot you brought with you", he ordered. But, the prisoner said, "Let them be here itself. I shall be coming back soon". That is the attitude of most people. They are reluctant to leave this prison house of earthly life. They do enough Karma in this life, to deserve another life-sentence and they come back pretty soon, to undergo the same.

THE MANGO

When the mango is tender on the tree, it is very unpleasant to the tongue, with an astringent taste. After some weeks, when it grows big, it will taste very sour. But, when it is fully ripe, it can be eaten with relish, for, the juice will be sweet and replete with pleasant flavour.

Man too is like the mango. The astringent stage is the early Thamasic stage--the stage of indolence, inactivity and dullness. Man must then be alert, not to be satisfied with sloth. He must dream of the consummation that is in store. Then, man attains the Rajasic stage as the mango reaches the sour stage. Man then enjoys power over others; he pursues vigorously the fancies of his senses and prides himself on his possessions. But, man must, at this stage be vigilant and pull himself back, in time, and gain control over his passions and prejudices. This will make him a sweet juicy ripe coveted 'mango', of the Satwic type.

AYODHYA FOR HIM

When Vibhishana, the Rakshasa Prince, the brother of the Arch-Enemy Ravana, came to the camp of Rama as a refugee, Rama accepted him, in spite of the protests of those around him. He said, "It is my unbreakable vow; I shall accept all who take refuge in me". He blessed Vibhishana with another act of Grace also: He crowned him the Emperor of Lanka, thereby asserting that Ravana, his elder brother, would lose both his throne and his life in the fight that was inevitable. At this, Sugriva expressed surprise, for, he said, "Lord! If tomorrow Ravana comes into camp and surrenders, and craves pardon for his misdemeanours, how can he be deprived by you, of Lanka and its throne? Rama smiled at his fears and replied, "My word can never fail. Vibhishana will be the Ruler of Lanka, whatever happens. If Ravana surrenders, I shall seat him on the throne of Ayodhya".

MILK AND WATER

Pour a glass of water into a vessel containing a hundred glasses of milk; the water you poured gets the properties of milk and fetches the price of milk. It improves by the association! Pour a glass of milk into a vessel containing a hundred glasses of water. The milk loses its health-giving sustaining properties and becomes as tasteless as water itself! This is the consequence of the company we mix in.

SAI BABA AND THE SCHOOL BOY

There was a schoolboy once who was very poor in mathematics. When the day of examination in Mathematics came round, he went to a temple of Sai Baba and vowed that, if the questions were easy and he could do all the sums correct, he could offer 5 kg. of sweetened rice to Him. The paper turned put to be quite within the limits of his capacity; he finished answering all the questions within 2 hours; the sums were all correctly solved; he had an extra hour on hand.

So, he took a few sheets of paper and drew up a list of items with their price, to prepare the offering he had vowed to Sai Baba. He had a ten-rupee note in his pocket; but, when he added up the cost of rice, sugar, cashewnut, cardamom, ghee, dried grapes etc., the total amount required was found to be about 15 rupees! He tried concealing a few items and reducing the quantities of a few, but the total was always more than what he could afford.

Then, he argued that Sai Baba was not in need of Sweetened rice and that a few fruits should certainly satisfy Him. Fruits too were pretty costly, he found; flowers were not so costly, but, he remembered that in Gita, God had said that pathram (leaf), pushpam (flower), phalam (fruit) or thoyam (water) would be enough to please Him. So, he finally decided that thoyam from the well in his house would be ample payment for the Grace he received that day. He could well save the tenner for a film he longed to see; he calculated how much that would cost and was glad to find that he could take to the picture one of his friends too. Just when he arrived at this happy conclusion, the invigilator called that the hour was over and asked

for the answer papers to be handed in.

Our friend woke up from his reverie and in the confusion, he handed over the sheets whereon he had made all the calculations of cost and quantity for the sweetened rice offering, the fruits and the flowers, and finally, the picture. When he went home and looked into the papers he had brought home he found to his dismay that they were the answer-papers he had to give the invigilator! It is all a matter of 'reaction, resound and reflection'. What you plan to do to another recoils on you. God is neither angry, not vengeful. He is the eternal witness of the play. You punish yourselves for your evil thoughts and deeds; you reward yourselves for your good thoughts and deeds. That is the real Truth.